ADHD Across the Lifespan: From Childhood to Adulthood

Elena Olivera

Copyright © 2024 Elena Olivera

All rights reserved.

Table of Contents

Introduction:

Understanding ADHD: An Overview

Attention Deficit Hyperactivity Disorder (ADHD) is a neurodevelopmental disorder that significantly impacts an individual's ability to focus, control impulses, and regulate activity levels appropriate to their age. ADHD is one of the most common mental health disorders diagnosed in children and often persists into adulthood, affecting various aspects of life, including education, employment, and relationships. This introduction aims to provide a comprehensive understanding of ADHD, its symptoms, diagnosis, and the importance of awareness and early intervention.

Historical Background

The concept of ADHD has evolved considerably over the years. Early descriptions of what we now recognize as ADHD date back to the late 18th century when Sir Alexander Crichton described a mental state characterized by an inability to focus and a restless mind. However, it wasn't until the early 20th century that ADHD began to be formally recognized in the medical community. In 1902, British pediatrician Sir George Frederic Still published a series of lectures describing a group of children with significant problems with sustained attention and self-regulation, which he attributed to a "defect of moral control."

Throughout the 20th century, the understanding of ADHD continued to evolve.

Chapter 1: Symptoms and Diagnosis

Core symptoms: inattention, hyperactivity, and impulsivity

Inattention

Inattention is one of the hallmark symptoms of ADHD and can significantly impair an individual's ability to function in various settings. Individuals with inattention often have difficulty sustaining focus, following through on tasks, and organizing activities. This can lead to numerous challenges, particularly in academic and occupational environments.

Key Features of Inattention:

1. **Difficulty Sustaining Attention**: Individuals with ADHD may struggle to maintain focus on tasks or activities, especially those that are repetitive or require prolonged mental effort. They may start projects or assignments but have difficulty completing them due to losing interest or becoming easily distracted.
2. **Careless Mistakes**: People with ADHD often make careless mistakes in schoolwork, work tasks, or other activities. These errors are typically due to overlooking details or rushing through tasks without careful review.
3. **Disorganization**: Inattention can lead to significant difficulties with organization. Individuals may have trouble keeping track of their belongings, maintaining orderly workspaces, or planning and prioritizing tasks. This can result in missed deadlines, misplaced items, and a general sense of chaos.
4. **Avoidance of Sustained Mental Effort**: Tasks that require sustained mental effort, such as reading lengthy materials or completing complex projects, can be particularly challenging for those with ADHD. They may avoid or procrastinate on

these tasks, leading to further difficulties in academic or work performance.

5. **Easily Distracted**: External stimuli, such as background noise, conversations, or visual distractions, can easily divert the attention of someone with ADHD. This can make it hard to stay focused on a single task, leading to frequent interruptions and incomplete work.

6. **Forgetfulness**: Forgetting daily tasks, appointments, or important responsibilities is common in individuals with ADHD. This forgetfulness can extend to missing deadlines, failing to follow through on commitments, and general difficulties in managing day-to-day activities.

Hyperactivity

Hyperactivity is another core symptom of ADHD, characterized by excessive motor activity and an inability to stay still or engage in activities quietly. While hyperactivity is more apparent in children, it can also manifest in adults, albeit often in less overt ways.

Key Features of Hyperactivity:

1. **Fidgeting and Squirming**: Individuals with ADHD often exhibit constant fidgeting with their hands or feet and may squirm in their seats. This restlessness can be particularly noticeable in structured settings, such as classrooms or meetings.

2. **Inability to Stay Seated**: In situations where remaining seated is expected, such as in school or during meals, individuals with ADHD may frequently leave their seats. They may feel the need to move around or engage in physical activities, even when it is inappropriate.

3. **Excessive Running or Climbing**: Children with ADHD may run or climb excessively, even in situations where such behavior is not suitable. This can lead to difficulties in

maintaining appropriate behavior in structured environments.

4. **Difficulty Engaging in Quiet Activities**: Individuals with ADHD often struggle to engage in leisure activities quietly. They may talk loudly, move around frequently, or find it challenging to relax and enjoy calm activities.

5. **Talking Excessively**: Excessive talking is a common symptom of hyperactivity. Individuals with ADHD may dominate conversations, speak out of turn, and have difficulty listening to others. This can lead to social difficulties and misunderstandings.

Impulsivity

Impulsivity is the third core symptom of ADHD, involving hasty actions that occur without forethought and that can have harmful consequences. Impulsivity can manifest in various ways, including difficulty waiting for one's turn, interrupting others, and making quick decisions without considering the long-term effects.

Key Features of Impulsivity:

1. **Blurting Out Answers**: Individuals with ADHD may frequently interrupt others by blurting out answers or comments before questions have been fully asked. This impulsive behavior can disrupt conversations and make it difficult to participate in group activities appropriately.

2. **Difficulty Waiting for Their Turn**: Impulsivity can make it challenging for individuals with ADHD to wait for their turn in games, conversations, or other activities. This impatience can lead to frustration and conflicts with peers.

3. **Interrupting or Intruding on Others**: People with ADHD may interrupt others during conversations or intrude on their activities without recognizing the

social boundaries. This behavior can strain relationships and lead to social isolation.

4. **Making Hasty Decisions**: Impulsivity often leads to making quick decisions without considering the potential consequences. This can result in risky behaviors, such as reckless driving, impulsive spending, or engaging in unsafe activities.

Impact of Core Symptoms

The core symptoms of inattention, hyperactivity, and impulsivity can significantly impact an individual's life. In academic settings, these symptoms can lead to poor academic performance, difficulties in following instructions, and challenges in maintaining focus during lessons. In the workplace, adults with ADHD may struggle with meeting deadlines, organizing tasks, and maintaining productivity.

Socially, these symptoms can affect relationships with peers, family members, and colleagues. Impulsive behaviors and difficulties in social interactions can lead to misunderstandings, conflicts, and social isolation. Additionally, the constant struggle to manage symptoms can result in low self-esteem, frustration, and emotional distress.

Diagnosis and Assessment

Diagnosing ADHD involves a comprehensive assessment process that includes gathering information from multiple sources, such as parents, teachers, and the individuals themselves. The assessment typically includes clinical interviews, behavior rating scales, and observations of behavior across different settings. The diagnostic criteria outlined in the DSM-5 are used to determine whether the symptoms meet the threshold for ADHD.

Treatment and Management

Managing ADHD often requires a multifaceted approach that includes behavioral interventions, educational support, medication, and psychosocial support.

1. **Behavioral Interventions**: Behavioral therapy can help individuals with ADHD develop strategies to manage their symptoms. Techniques such as positive reinforcement, behavior modification, and parent training can be effective in reducing disruptive behaviors and improving functioning.
2. **Educational Support**: Schools can provide accommodations and modifications to support students with ADHD. Individualized Education Programs (IEPs) and 504 Plans can help create a supportive learning environment tailored to the needs of students with ADHD.
3. **Medication**: Stimulant medications, such as methylphenidate and amphetamines, are commonly prescribed to manage ADHD symptoms. Non-stimulant medications, such as atomoxetine and guanfacine, may also be used. These medications can help improve focus, reduce hyperactivity, and control impulsive behaviors.
4. **Psychosocial Support**: Support groups, counseling, and coaching can provide valuable assistance to individuals with ADHD and their families. These resources offer guidance, emotional support, and practical strategies for managing the challenges associated with ADHD.

Diagnostic criteria (DSM-5)

The Diagnostic and Statistical Manual of Mental Disorders, Fifth Edition (DSM-5), published by the American Psychiatric Association (APA), provides the standard criteria for diagnosing Attention Deficit Hyperactivity Disorder (ADHD). The DSM-5 outlines specific symptoms, duration, and functional impairments required to make a diagnosis. Understanding these criteria is crucial for clinicians, educators, and researchers in accurately identifying and managing ADHD.

Core Criteria for ADHD Diagnosis

The DSM-5 categorizes ADHD symptoms into two primary domains: inattention and hyperactivity-impulsivity. To diagnose ADHD, an individual must meet the criteria for one or both domains. The DSM-5 specifies that several symptoms must be present before the age of 12 and must occur in two or more settings (e.g., at home, school, or work). The symptoms must also cause significant impairment in social, academic, or occupational functioning and must not be better explained by another mental disorder.

Inattention Criteria

For a diagnosis of ADHD, predominantly inattentive presentation, an individual must exhibit at least six of the following symptoms (five for individuals 17 years and older) for at least six months:

1.   **Careless Mistakes**: Often fails to give close attention to details or makes careless mistakes in schoolwork, work, or other activities.

2. **Sustaining Attention**: Often has difficulty sustaining attention in tasks or play activities.
3. **Listening**: Often does not seem to listen when spoken to directly.
4. **Following Through**: Often does not follow through on instructions and fails to finish schoolwork, chores, or duties in the workplace (not due to oppositional behavior or failure to understand instructions).
5. **Organizing Tasks**: Often has difficulty organizing tasks and activities.
6. **Avoiding Sustained Mental Effort**: Often avoids, dislikes, or is reluctant to engage in tasks that require sustained mental effort (e.g., schoolwork, homework).
7. **Losing Items**: Often loses things necessary for tasks or activities (e.g., toys, school assignments, pencils, books, tools).
8. **Easily Distracted**: Is often easily distracted by extraneous stimuli.
9. **Forgetfulness**: Is often forgetful in daily activities.

Hyperactivity and Impulsivity Criteria

For a diagnosis of ADHD, predominantly hyperactive-impulsive presentation, an individual must exhibit at least six of the following symptoms (five for individuals 17 years and older) for at least six months:

1. **Fidgeting**: Often fidgets with or taps hands or feet or squirms in seat.
2. **Remaining Seated**: Often leaves seat in situations when remaining seated is expected.
3. **Running or Climbing**: Often runs about or climbs in situations where it is inappropriate (adolescents or adults may be limited to feeling restless).
4. **Quiet Activities**: Often unable to play or engage in leisure activities quietly.
5. **"On the Go"**: Is often "on the go," acting as if "driven by a motor."
6. **Talking Excessively**: Often talks excessively.

7. **Blurting Out**: Often blurts out an answer before a question has been completed.
8. **Difficulty Waiting**: Often has difficulty waiting their turn.
9. **Interrupting**: Often interrupts or intrudes on others (e.g., butts into conversations or games).

Combined Presentation

For a diagnosis of ADHD, combined presentation, an individual must meet the criteria for both inattention and hyperactivity-impulsivity domains. This means exhibiting at least six symptoms (five for those 17 years and older) from both categories for at least six months.

Additional Criteria

In addition to the symptom criteria, the DSM-5 includes the following considerations for a diagnosis of ADHD:

1. **Age of Onset**: Several symptoms must have been present before age 12. This criterion ensures that ADHD is recognized as a neurodevelopmental disorder typically manifesting early in life.
2. **Settings**: Several symptoms must be present in two or more settings (e.g., at home, school, or work). This criterion helps distinguish ADHD from situational or contextual issues, ensuring that symptoms are pervasive and not limited to one environment.
3. **Impairment**: There must be clear evidence that the symptoms interfere with, or reduce the quality of, social, academic, or occupational functioning. This criterion emphasizes that ADHD symptoms must

cause significant difficulties in the individual's daily life.

4. **Differential Diagnosis**: The symptoms must not be better explained by another mental disorder, such as mood disorders, anxiety disorders, dissociative disorders, or personality disorders. This criterion ensures that the diagnosis is specific to ADHD and not a manifestation of another condition.

Developmental Considerations

The presentation of ADHD symptoms can vary with age. In young children, hyperactivity-impulsivity symptoms are often more prominent, whereas in older children and adults, inattention tends to be more evident. Adolescents and adults may exhibit symptoms in more subtle ways, such as restlessness rather than overt hyperactivity, and may struggle more with organizational tasks and time management.

Gender Differences

Boys are more frequently diagnosed with ADHD than girls, possibly due to differences in symptom presentation. Boys often exhibit more hyperactive and impulsive behaviors, which are more noticeable and disruptive. Girls, on the other hand, may display more inattentive symptoms, which can be less overt and sometimes overlooked. Understanding these gender differences is essential for accurate diagnosis and intervention.

Cultural Considerations

Cultural factors can influence the recognition and diagnosis of ADHD. Different cultures may have varying expectations for behavior and levels of tolerance for inattentiveness and hyperactivity. Additionally, access to healthcare and educational resources can affect the likelihood of diagnosis and treatment. Clinicians must be culturally sensitive and consider these factors when evaluating individuals for ADHD.

Importance of Accurate Diagnosis

Accurate diagnosis of ADHD is crucial for several reasons:

1. **Appropriate Treatment**: Identifying ADHD correctly allows for appropriate treatment planning, which can include behavioral interventions, educational support, and medication management. Early and accurate diagnosis can lead to better outcomes and improved quality of life.
2. **Avoiding Misdiagnosis**: Misdiagnosing ADHD can lead to inappropriate treatments and interventions that may not address the underlying issues. It can also prevent individuals from receiving the necessary support for their actual condition.
3. **Educational and Occupational Accommodations**: A proper diagnosis can facilitate access to educational and workplace accommodations, such as extended test-taking time, organizational support, and modifications

to work tasks, helping individuals succeed in their academic and professional endeavors.

Conditions Commonly Confused with ADHD

1. **Anxiety Disorders**
2. **Depressive Disorders**
3. **Bipolar Disorder**
4. **Oppositional Defiant Disorder (ODD)**
5. **Conduct Disorder**
6. **Autism Spectrum Disorder (ASD)**
7. **Learning Disabilities**
8. **Sensory Processing Disorder**
9. **Sleep Disorders**
10. **Trauma and Stressor-Related Disorders**

Anxiety Disorders

Similarities to ADHD:

- Difficulty concentrating
- Restlessness
- Irritability

Key Differences:

- Anxiety disorders primarily involve excessive fear and worry. Individuals with anxiety may appear inattentive because they are preoccupied with their worries, whereas those with ADHD struggle with inattention across various contexts.

- Physical symptoms such as stomachaches, headaches, and muscle tension are more common in anxiety disorders.
- Anxiety-related behaviors often worsen in specific situations that trigger the individual's fears, while ADHD symptoms are more consistent across different settings.

Diagnostic Considerations:

- Assess for specific anxiety symptoms such as excessive worry, panic attacks, and phobias.
- Consider using anxiety-specific rating scales and structured interviews.
- Evaluate the temporal relationship between inattention and anxiety symptoms.

Depressive Disorders

Similarities to ADHD:

- Difficulty concentrating
- Fatigue
- Irritability

Key Differences:

- Depressive disorders are characterized by persistent sadness, loss of interest or pleasure in activities, and other mood-related symptoms.
- Inattention in depression is often related to a lack of motivation and low energy, whereas in ADHD, it is more related to distractibility and difficulty sustaining focus.
- Depressive symptoms, such as changes in appetite and sleep patterns, are less common in ADHD.

Diagnostic Considerations:

- Assess for core depressive symptoms such as persistent low mood, anhedonia, and feelings of hopelessness.
- Use depression-specific rating scales and clinical interviews.
- Evaluate the duration and context of the inattention and mood symptoms.

Bipolar Disorder

Similarities to ADHD:

- Hyperactivity
- Impulsivity
- Mood swings

Key Differences:

- Bipolar disorder is characterized by distinct mood episodes, including manic, hypomanic, and depressive episodes. These episodes are typically episodic and cyclical, whereas ADHD symptoms are more chronic and consistent.
- During manic episodes, individuals may exhibit grandiosity, decreased need for sleep, and risky behaviors, which are not typical of ADHD.
- ADHD does not involve the severe mood elevation seen in bipolar disorder.

Diagnostic Considerations:

- Assess for the presence of distinct mood episodes, including their duration and frequency.
- Use mood disorder-specific rating scales and diagnostic interviews.
- Evaluate family history, as bipolar disorder has a strong genetic component.

Oppositional Defiant Disorder (ODD)

Similarities to ADHD:

- Defiance
- Irritability
- Impulsivity

Key Differences:

- ODD is primarily characterized by a pattern of angry, irritable mood, argumentative/defiant behavior, and vindictiveness.
- Individuals with ODD may specifically exhibit oppositional behavior towards authority figures, whereas those with ADHD may be inattentive and impulsive across various contexts.
- The behavioral issues in ODD are more related to emotional regulation and interpersonal conflicts, whereas ADHD involves broader difficulties with attention and impulse control.

Diagnostic Considerations:

- Assess for a pattern of oppositional and defiant behaviors, including their context and frequency.
- Use behavior-specific rating scales and structured interviews.
- Evaluate the relationship between inattentive and oppositional behaviors.

Conduct Disorder

Similarities to ADHD:

- Impulsivity
- Defiant behavior
- Academic difficulties

Key Differences:

- Conduct disorder involves a persistent pattern of behavior that violates societal norms and the rights of others, including aggression, theft, and serious rule violations.
- ADHD-related impulsivity does not typically include the deliberate harmful or illegal behaviors seen in conduct disorder.
- Conduct disorder is more associated with antisocial behaviors and a lack of empathy or remorse.

Diagnostic Considerations:

- Assess for a pattern of serious rule violations, aggressive behaviors, and deceitfulness.
- Use conduct disorder-specific rating scales and diagnostic interviews.
- Evaluate the presence of co-occurring disorders, as conduct disorder often coexists with ADHD.

Autism Spectrum Disorder (ASD)

Similarities to ADHD:

- Difficulty concentrating
- Social difficulties
- Hyperactivity

Key Differences:

- ASD is characterized by persistent deficits in social communication and interaction, along with restricted, repetitive patterns of behavior, interests, or activities.
- Social difficulties in ASD involve challenges with social reciprocity, nonverbal communication, and developing relationships, which are distinct from the inattentiveness and impulsivity of ADHD.

- Repetitive behaviors and narrow interests are more typical of ASD.

Diagnostic Considerations:

- Assess for core ASD symptoms, including social communication deficits and repetitive behaviors.
- Use autism-specific rating scales and structured diagnostic tools.
- Consider developmental history, as ASD symptoms are often noticeable in early childhood.

Learning Disabilities

Similarities to ADHD:

- Academic difficulties
- Inattention
- Poor organizational skills

Key Differences:

- Learning disabilities are specific impairments in reading, writing, or mathematics that are not due to a lack of intelligence or inadequate instruction.
- Inattention in learning disabilities is often task-specific and related to difficulties in processing specific types of information, whereas ADHD-related inattention is more pervasive.
- ADHD symptoms include broader issues with impulse control and hyperactivity, which are not typical of learning disabilities.

Diagnostic Considerations:

- Assess for specific learning difficulties using standardized academic achievement tests.
- Use cognitive assessments to identify processing deficits.

- Evaluate the consistency of inattentive symptoms across various academic and non-academic tasks.

Sensory Processing Disorder

Similarities to ADHD:

- Hyperactivity
- Difficulty focusing
- Restlessness

Key Differences:

- Sensory Processing Disorder involves difficulties in processing and responding to sensory stimuli, leading to over- or under-responsiveness to sensory input.
- Hyperactivity in sensory processing disorder is often related to sensory-seeking behaviors, whereas ADHD-related hyperactivity is due to general restlessness and impulsivity.
- Sensory processing issues can lead to specific aversions or attractions to sensory experiences, which are less common in ADHD.

Diagnostic Considerations:

- Assess for sensory processing difficulties using sensory-specific assessments and questionnaires.
- Observe the individual's response to various sensory stimuli.
- Evaluate the impact of sensory processing issues on daily functioning.

Sleep Disorders

Similarities to ADHD:

- Inattention

- Hyperactivity
- Irritability

Key Differences:

- Sleep disorders, such as sleep apnea or insomnia, can cause daytime fatigue, inattention, and irritability due to poor sleep quality.
- ADHD symptoms are present regardless of sleep quality, while sleep disorder-related symptoms may improve with adequate rest.
- Sleep disorders often involve specific sleep-related symptoms, such as snoring, difficulty falling or staying asleep, and excessive daytime sleepiness.

Diagnostic Considerations:

- Assess for sleep-related symptoms and patterns using sleep questionnaires and diaries.
- Consider a sleep study to identify underlying sleep disorders.
- Evaluate the relationship between sleep quality and daytime symptoms.

Trauma and Stressor-Related Disorders

Similarities to ADHD:

- Difficulty concentrating
- Hypervigilance
- Irritability

Key Differences:

- Trauma and stressor-related disorders, such as Post-Traumatic Stress Disorder (PTSD), involve symptoms related to a traumatic event, including re-experiencing the trauma, avoidance, and hyperarousal.

- Inattention and hyperactivity in trauma-related disorders are often situational and linked to trauma reminders, whereas ADHD symptoms are more consistent.
- Trauma-related symptoms include flashbacks, nightmares, and heightened startle response, which are not typical of ADHD.

Diagnostic Considerations:

- Assess for history of trauma and specific trauma-related symptoms.
- Use trauma-specific assessment tools and clinical interviews.
- Consider the temporal relationship between trauma exposure and the onset of symptoms.

Chapter 2: Types of ADHD

Predominantly Inattentive Presentation

Diagnostic Criteria for Predominantly Inattentive Presentation

According to the DSM-5, an individual must exhibit at least six of the following symptoms of inattention (five for those aged 17 and older) for at least six months, to a degree that is inconsistent with developmental level and that negatively impacts social, academic, or occupational activities:

1. **Careless Mistakes**: Often fails to give close attention to details or makes careless mistakes in schoolwork, work, or other activities.
2. **Sustaining Attention**: Often has difficulty sustaining attention in tasks or play activities.
3. **Listening**: Often does not seem to listen when spoken to directly.
4. **Following Through**: Often does not follow through on instructions and fails to finish schoolwork, chores, or duties in the workplace.

5. **Organizing Tasks**: Often has difficulty organizing tasks and activities.
6. **Avoiding Sustained Mental Effort**: Often avoids, dislikes, or is reluctant to engage in tasks that require sustained mental effort.
7. **Losing Items**: Often loses things necessary for tasks or activities (e.g., toys, school assignments, pencils, books, tools).
8. **Easily Distracted**: Is often easily distracted by extraneous stimuli.
9. **Forgetfulness**: Is often forgetful in daily activities.

Key Characteristics and Symptoms

Inattention

Individuals with the Predominantly Inattentive Presentation of ADHD primarily struggle with maintaining focus, organizing tasks, and following through on assignments. These difficulties are evident in various settings, including academic, occupational, and social environments.

Core Symptoms:

- **Careless Mistakes**: This symptom reflects a tendency to overlook details, resulting in frequent errors in schoolwork, work tasks, or other activities. This isn't due to a lack of knowledge or skill but rather an inability to maintain consistent attention to detail.
- **Difficulty Sustaining Attention**: Individuals may find it hard to stay focused during lectures, conversations, or lengthy reading materials. Their mind may wander, leading to incomplete tasks and difficulty absorbing information.
- **Listening Problems**: Often, individuals appear not to listen when spoken to directly. This isn't due to defiance or lack of understanding but a frequent zoning out or becoming preoccupied with other thoughts.

- **Challenges in Following Through**: This involves starting tasks but not completing them. Individuals may begin assignments or chores but fail to finish due to losing interest or becoming distracted by other activities.
- **Organizational Difficulties**: Keeping track of tasks and managing time efficiently is often a significant challenge. This can lead to missed deadlines, forgotten appointments, and a general sense of disorganization.
- **Avoidance of Sustained Mental Effort**: Tasks that require prolonged concentration, such as studying for exams, writing reports, or completing homework, are often avoided or put off. This avoidance is due to the mental effort these tasks require, which can be exhausting for those with ADHD.
- **Losing Items**: Frequently misplacing items necessary for tasks or daily activities is common. This can include school supplies, personal belongings, or important documents.
- **Easily Distracted**: External stimuli, such as noises, conversations, or even internal thoughts, can easily divert attention away from the task at hand. This makes it difficult to stay focused on one activity for an extended period.
- **Forgetfulness**: Forgetting daily activities, appointments, or important tasks is a hallmark of this presentation. This forgetfulness is not intentional but rather a result of the cognitive challenges associated with ADHD.

Impact on Daily Life

The symptoms of the Predominantly Inattentive Presentation can significantly impact various aspects of an individual's life:

1. **Academic Performance**: Students may struggle with completing assignments, following through on

instructions, and staying focused during classes. This can lead to lower grades, academic underachievement, and negative feedback from teachers.

2. **Occupational Functioning**: Adults with this presentation may find it difficult to meet deadlines, organize tasks, and maintain productivity at work. This can result in job dissatisfaction, underperformance, and strained relationships with colleagues and supervisors.

3. **Social Interactions**: Difficulty paying attention during conversations and forgetting social plans can strain friendships and relationships. Individuals may be perceived as disinterested or unreliable, leading to social isolation or conflicts.

4. **Daily Activities**: Managing daily responsibilities, such as paying bills, maintaining a household, and keeping track of appointments, can be challenging. This can lead to financial difficulties, disorganized living environments, and missed medical or social appointments.

Differential Diagnosis

Accurately diagnosing the Predominantly Inattentive Presentation of ADHD requires differentiating it from other conditions with similar symptoms:

- **Anxiety Disorders**: Both conditions can involve difficulties with concentration and restlessness. However, anxiety disorders are characterized by excessive worry and fear, which are not primary features of ADHD.
- **Depressive Disorders**: Depression can lead to concentration problems and low motivation.

However, depression involves persistent sadness, loss of interest in activities, and other mood-related symptoms that are not central to ADHD.

- **Learning Disabilities**: Learning disabilities involve specific difficulties with reading, writing, or mathematics. ADHD symptoms are more pervasive and not limited to academic tasks.
- **Autism Spectrum Disorder (ASD)**: ASD can involve inattention and social difficulties. However, ASD is characterized by deficits in social communication and repetitive behaviors, which are not features of ADHD.
- **Sensory Processing Disorder**: Sensory processing issues can lead to distractibility and hyperactivity. However, these behaviors are linked to sensory stimuli, whereas ADHD-related inattention is more general.

Diagnosis and Assessment

Diagnosing the Predominantly Inattentive Presentation involves a comprehensive evaluation, including:

1. **Clinical Interviews**: Gathering detailed information about the individual's symptoms, history, and impact on daily functioning from multiple sources (e.g., self-reports, parents, teachers).
2. **Behavior Rating Scales**: Using standardized rating scales to assess the frequency and severity of ADHD symptoms.
3. **Observation**: Direct observation of behavior in various settings, such as home,

school, or workplace, can provide valuable insights into the individual's challenges.

4. **Medical Evaluation**: Ruling out other medical conditions that might explain the symptoms, such as thyroid disorders or sleep apnea.

Treatment and Management

Effective management of the Predominantly Inattentive Presentation of ADHD typically involves a combination of strategies:

1. **Behavioral Interventions**: Behavioral therapy can help individuals develop skills to manage their symptoms. Techniques such as cognitive-behavioral therapy (CBT) can address organizational skills, time management, and coping strategies.
2. **Educational Support**: Schools can provide accommodations such as extended test time, preferential seating, and organizational support. Individualized Education Programs (IEPs) or 504 Plans can tailor educational approaches to the student's needs.
3. **Medication**: Stimulant medications (e.g., methylphenidate, amphetamines) and non-stimulant medications (e.g., atomoxetine) can improve attention and reduce distractibility. Medication decisions should be made in consultation with a healthcare provider, considering potential benefits and side effects.
4. **Psychoeducation**: Educating individuals and their families about ADHD can foster understanding and develop effective coping strategies. This includes learning about the nature of the disorder, treatment options, and techniques for managing symptoms.

5. **Support Groups**: Connecting with others who have similar experiences can provide emotional support, practical advice, and a sense of community.

Predominantly Hyperactive-Impulsive Presentation

Diagnostic Criteria for Predominantly Hyperactive-Impulsive Presentation

The DSM-5 outlines specific criteria for diagnosing the Predominantly Hyperactive-Impulsive Presentation of ADHD. An individual must exhibit at least six of the following symptoms (five for those aged 17 and older) for at least six months, to a degree that is inconsistent with developmental level and that negatively impacts social, academic, or occupational activities:

1. **Fidgeting**: Often fidgets with or taps hands or feet or squirms in seat.
2. **Remaining Seated**: Often leaves seat in situations when remaining seated is expected.
3. **Running or Climbing**: Often runs about or climbs in situations where it is inappropriate (adolescents or adults may be limited to feeling restless).
4. **Quiet Activities**: Often unable to play or engage in leisure activities quietly.
5. **"On the Go"**: Is often "on the go," acting as if "driven by a motor."
6. **Talking Excessively**: Often talks excessively.
7. **Blurting Out**: Often blurts out an answer before a question has been completed.
8. **Difficulty Waiting**: Often has difficulty waiting their turn.
9. **Interrupting**: Often interrupts or intrudes on others (e.g., butts into conversations or games).

Key Characteristics and Symptoms

Hyperactivity

Individuals with the Predominantly Hyperactive-Impulsive Presentation primarily exhibit behaviors that indicate excessive energy and difficulty staying still or quiet. These behaviors are often noticeable and can be disruptive in various settings.
Core Symptoms:

- **Fidgeting and Squirming**: Constant movement of hands or feet, tapping, or squirming in the seat. This behavior is often uncontrollable and noticeable in situations that require sitting still, such as classrooms or meetings.
- **Difficulty Remaining Seated**: Frequently getting up when it is expected to remain seated, such as during class, at the dinner table, or in meetings. This can lead to frequent disruptions and difficulties in structured environments.
- **Running or Climbing Inappropriately**: Engaging in physical activities like running or climbing in settings where it is not appropriate, such as a classroom or an office. In older individuals, this may manifest as feelings of restlessness or the need to move constantly.
- **Difficulty Engaging in Quiet Activities**: Struggling to participate in activities that require calmness and quiet, such as reading or playing quiet games. This can lead to avoidance of such activities or inability to engage in them without causing disruption.
- **Being "On the Go"**: Exhibiting a constant state of activity, as if driven by a motor. This can make the individual seem perpetually restless and unable to relax or slow down.

- **Excessive Talking**: Talking more than is appropriate in social contexts, often without considering the appropriateness of the timing or setting. This can include interrupting others or dominating conversations.

Impulsivity

Impulsivity involves acting without forethought or consideration of consequences. Individuals with this presentation often struggle with self-control, leading to spontaneous and sometimes risky behaviors.

Core Symptoms:

- **Blurting Out Answers**: Answering questions before they have been fully asked, often interrupting the speaker. This can be particularly problematic in academic settings, leading to classroom disruptions.
- **Difficulty Waiting**: Struggling to wait for one's turn in various contexts, such as during games, in lines, or in conversations. This impatience can lead to frustration and conflicts with others.
- **Interrupting or Intruding**: Frequently interrupting or intruding on others' activities or conversations. This behavior can be perceived as rude or disrespectful, straining social interactions and relationships.

Impact on Daily Life

The symptoms of the Predominantly Hyperactive-Impulsive Presentation can significantly impact various aspects of an individual's life:

1. **Academic Performance**: Students may struggle to sit still, follow classroom rules, or wait their

turn to speak. This can lead to frequent disciplinary actions, negative feedback from teachers, and academic underperformance.

2. **Occupational Functioning**: Adults with this presentation may find it challenging to adhere to workplace norms, such as remaining seated during meetings, completing tasks that require sustained attention, or interacting appropriately with colleagues. This can result in job dissatisfaction, conflicts with supervisors, and underachievement.

3. **Social Interactions**: Difficulty waiting, interrupting others, and excessive talking can strain relationships with peers, family members, and partners. Individuals may be perceived as disruptive, impatient, or inconsiderate, leading to social isolation or conflicts.

4. **Daily Activities**: Managing daily responsibilities, such as driving, following schedules, or engaging in leisure activities, can be challenging. Impulsivity can lead to risky behaviors, while hyperactivity can result in a constant need for activity and movement.

Differential Diagnosis

Accurately diagnosing the Predominantly Hyperactive-Impulsive Presentation requires differentiating it from other conditions with similar symptoms:

- **Oppositional Defiant Disorder (ODD)**: ODD involves a pattern of angry, irritable mood, argumentative/defiant behavior, and vindictiveness. Unlike ADHD, the behavior in ODD is primarily directed at authority figures and involves a deliberate refusal to comply with rules.

- **Conduct Disorder**: This disorder includes a pattern of behavior that violates societal norms and the rights of others, such as aggression, theft, and serious rule violations. ADHD-related impulsivity does not typically include the intentional harmful or illegal behaviors seen in conduct disorder.
- **Bipolar Disorder**: Bipolar disorder is characterized by distinct mood episodes, including manic or hypomanic episodes. During these episodes, individuals may exhibit hyperactivity, impulsivity, and risky behaviors, similar to ADHD. However, bipolar disorder involves cyclical mood changes, whereas ADHD symptoms are more consistent.
- **Autism Spectrum Disorder (ASD)**: ASD can involve hyperactivity and impulsivity. However, ASD is primarily characterized by deficits in social communication and repetitive behaviors. Social difficulties in ASD are related to challenges in understanding social cues, whereas in ADHD, they are due to impulsive and hyperactive behaviors.
- **Anxiety Disorders**: Anxiety can lead to restlessness and difficulty concentrating, similar to hyperactivity. However, anxiety is primarily driven by excessive worry and fear, which are not core features of ADHD.

Diagnosis and Assessment

Diagnosing the Predominantly Hyperactive-Impulsive Presentation involves a comprehensive evaluation, including:

1. **Clinical Interviews**: Gathering detailed information about the individual's symptoms, history, and impact on daily functioning from multiple sources (e.g., self-reports, parents, teachers).
2. **Behavior Rating Scales**: Using standardized rating scales to assess the frequency and severity of ADHD symptoms.
3. **Observation**: Direct observation of behavior in various settings, such as home, school, or workplace, can provide valuable insights into the individual's challenges.
4. **Medical Evaluation**: Ruling out other medical conditions that might explain the symptoms, such as thyroid disorders or sleep apnea.

Treatment and Management

Effective management of the Predominantly Hyperactive-Impulsive Presentation of ADHD typically involves a combination of strategies:

1. **Behavioral Interventions**: Behavioral therapy can help individuals develop skills to manage their symptoms. Techniques such as cognitive-behavioral therapy (CBT) can address impulsivity, hyperactivity, and social skills.
2. **Educational Support**: Schools can provide accommodations such as seating arrangements that minimize distractions, providing breaks for physical activity, and structured routines. Individualized Education Programs (IEPs) or 504 Plans can tailor educational approaches to the student's needs.

3. **Medication**: Stimulant medications (e.g., methylphenidate, amphetamines) and non-stimulant medications (e.g., atomoxetine) can reduce hyperactivity and impulsivity. Medication decisions should be made in consultation with a healthcare provider, considering potential benefits and side effects.
4. **Psychoeducation**: Educating individuals and their families about ADHD can foster understanding and develop effective coping strategies. This includes learning about the nature of the disorder, treatment options, and techniques for managing symptoms.
5. **Support Groups**: Connecting with others who have similar experiences can provide emotional support, practical advice, and a sense of community.
6. **Lifestyle Modifications**: Encouraging regular physical activity, structured routines, and healthy sleep habits can help manage symptoms. Physical activities can provide an outlet for excess energy and improve overall well-being.

Chapter 3: Causes and Risk Factors

Genetic influences

Studies have consistently demonstrated a strong genetic component in ADHD, with heritability estimates ranging from 70% to 80%. This suggests that genetic factors contribute substantially to individual differences in ADHD symptoms and susceptibility to the disorder. Twin studies have provided compelling evidence for the heritability of ADHD, showing higher concordance rates for ADHD among identical twins compared to fraternal twins.

Candidate Genes

Numerous candidate genes have been implicated in ADHD, with research focusing on genes involved in neurotransmitter signaling, neurodevelopmental processes, and executive functioning. Some of the key genes associated with ADHD include:

1. **DRD4 (Dopamine Receptor D4)**: Variants of the DRD4 gene have been linked to ADHD, particularly those associated with reduced dopamine receptor sensitivity. Dopamine plays a crucial role in reward processing, attention regulation, and motor control, making it a prime candidate for ADHD susceptibility.
2. **DRD5 (Dopamine Receptor D5)**: Similar to DRD4, variants of the DRD5 gene have been associated with ADHD, albeit with less consistent findings. Dopamine receptor genes are involved in modulating dopaminergic activity in the brain, which is dysregulated in ADHD.
3. **DAT1 (Dopamine Transporter)**: The DAT1 gene encodes the dopamine transporter, which regulates dopamine reuptake from the synaptic cleft. Variants of DAT1 have been implicated in ADHD, affecting dopamine clearance and synaptic dopamine levels.
4. **COMT (Catechol-O-Methyltransferase)**: The COMT gene encodes an enzyme involved in dopamine metabolism. Variants of COMT influence dopamine degradation, with the Val158Met polymorphism being associated with ADHD susceptibility.
5. **ADHD Candidate Gene 6 (ADHD6)**: This gene has been identified through genome-wide association studies (GWAS) as a potential risk factor for ADHD. Its specific role in ADHD pathophysiology is still being elucidated.

Polygenic Risk Scores

Recent advancements in genetic research, particularly genome-wide association studies (GWAS), have enabled the identification of multiple genetic variants associated with ADHD. Polygenic risk scores (PRS) aggregate information from these genetic variants to calculate an individual's genetic predisposition to ADHD. Higher PRS scores indicate a greater genetic risk for ADHD and have been associated with increased ADHD symptom severity and impairment.

Gene-Environment Interactions

While genetic factors contribute significantly to ADHD susceptibility, interactions between genes and environmental factors also play a crucial role. Prenatal exposure to maternal smoking, alcohol consumption, and environmental toxins can interact with genetic vulnerabilities to increase the risk of ADHD. Additionally, psychosocial stressors such as family dysfunction, socioeconomic disadvantage, and early adversity can exacerbate genetic predispositions to ADHD.

Implications for Treatment and Intervention

Understanding the genetic basis of ADHD holds promise for the development of targeted interventions and personalized treatment approaches. Pharmacogenetic studies aim to identify genetic markers that predict individual responses to ADHD medications, allowing for more precise medication selection and dosing. Furthermore, insights into the neurobiological pathways implicated in ADHD may inform the development of novel therapeutics targeting specific molecular mechanisms.

Environmental factors

Prenatal and Perinatal Factors

1. **Maternal Smoking and Substance Use**: Prenatal exposure to tobacco smoke, alcohol, and illicit drugs has been consistently linked to an increased risk of ADHD in offspring. Nicotine and other substances can disrupt fetal neurodevelopment, leading to alterations in brain structure and function associated with ADHD symptoms.
2. **Maternal Stress and Depression**: Maternal stress during pregnancy, as well as maternal depression and anxiety, have been identified as risk factors for ADHD in children. Stress-related hormones and inflammatory markers may impact fetal brain development, contributing to ADHD susceptibility.
3. **Prenatal Nutrition**: Maternal diet during pregnancy, including deficiencies in essential nutrients such as omega-3 fatty acids and iron, has been implicated in ADHD risk. Adequate prenatal nutrition is crucial for optimal brain development and may mitigate the risk of ADHD-related impairments.
4. **Complications During Birth**: Perinatal complications such as premature birth, low birth weight, hypoxia, and birth trauma have been associated with an increased likelihood of developing ADHD. These complications can disrupt normal brain maturation processes and increase susceptibility to neurodevelopmental disorders.

Early Childhood Factors

1. **Exposure to Environmental Toxins**: Environmental toxins such as lead, mercury, polychlorinated biphenyls (PCBs), and pesticides have been linked to ADHD risk. These substances can interfere with neurotransmitter systems, disrupt neuronal signaling pathways, and impair cognitive and behavioral functioning.
2. **Parenting Practices**: Inconsistent or harsh parenting practices, characterized by high levels of criticism, hostility, and punitive discipline, have been associated with ADHD symptoms in children. Positive parenting strategies that promote warmth, consistency, and effective discipline may mitigate ADHD-related impairments.
3. **Family Dysfunction and Adversity**: Adverse family environments, including parental marital conflict, family instability, and socioeconomic disadvantage, have been linked to ADHD risk. Family stressors can contribute to emotional dysregulation, impaired self-control, and behavioral problems characteristic of ADHD.
4. **Early Adversity and Trauma**: Exposure to early adversity, including maltreatment, neglect, and trauma, has been identified as a risk factor for ADHD. Adverse childhood experiences can disrupt stress response systems, alter brain development, and increase susceptibility to psychiatric disorders.

School and Socioeconomic Factors

1. **Educational Disadvantage**: Inadequate educational resources, overcrowded classrooms, and ineffective teaching methods may exacerbate ADHD symptoms and impair academic functioning. Educational

interventions that provide additional support, accommodations, and individualized instruction can help mitigate the impact of ADHD on academic performance.

2. **Peer Relationships and Social Exclusion**: Peer rejection, social isolation, and bullying victimization are common experiences for children with ADHD and can exacerbate social difficulties and emotional distress. Positive peer relationships and social support networks are essential for promoting social competence and psychological well-being.

3. **Socioeconomic Disparities**: Socioeconomic disadvantage, characterized by poverty, unemployment, and lack of access to healthcare and social services, is associated with an increased risk of ADHD. Socioeconomic disparities contribute to environmental stressors, inadequate parental support, and limited opportunities for enrichment and stimulation.

Media and Technology Exposure

1. **Screen Time and Digital Media**: Excessive screen time and media exposure, including television, video games, and electronic devices, have been linked to ADHD symptoms and attention difficulties in children. Prolonged screen time can disrupt sleep patterns, impair attentional control, and exacerbate behavioral problems.

2. **Social Media and Internet Use**: Social media use and internet addiction have been associated with ADHD-related impairments in adolescents and young adults. Excessive use of social media platforms, online gaming, and

digital communication may contribute to attentional difficulties, impulsivity, and addictive behaviors.

Brain structure and function

Brain Anatomy

1. **Prefrontal Cortex (PFC)**: The prefrontal cortex, particularly the dorsolateral prefrontal cortex (DLPFC) and ventrolateral prefrontal cortex (VLPFC), plays a central role in executive functions such as attention regulation, inhibitory control, and working memory. Structural abnormalities, including reduced volume and altered cortical thickness, have been observed in the PFC of individuals with ADHD, contributing to deficits in executive functioning.
2. **Basal Ganglia**: The basal ganglia, including the caudate nucleus, putamen, and globus pallidus, are involved in motor control, reward processing, and inhibitory control. Dysregulation of dopaminergic signaling within the basal ganglia is implicated in ADHD, with structural alterations and functional abnormalities observed in these regions.
3. **Cerebellum**: The cerebellum, traditionally associated with motor coordination, also plays a role in cognitive processes such as attention and timing. Structural abnormalities in the cerebellum, including reduced volume and alterations in connectivity, have been reported in individuals with ADHD, contributing to deficits in attentional control and timing.
4. **Corpus Callosum**: The corpus callosum, which facilitates communication between the brain's hemispheres, exhibits alterations in structure and connectivity in individuals with ADHD. Reduced corpus callosum volume and disrupted interhemispheric connectivity may contribute to impairments in attentional control and integration of cognitive processes.

Brain Connectivity

1. **Fronto-Striatal Circuitry**: Dysfunction within fronto-striatal circuits, encompassing connections between the PFC and basal ganglia, is implicated in ADHD. Altered connectivity and aberrant functional integration within these circuits contribute to deficits in inhibitory control, reward processing, and motor coordination observed in individuals with ADHD.
2. **Default Mode Network (DMN)**: The default mode network, involved in self-referential processing and mind-wandering, exhibits atypical connectivity patterns in individuals with ADHD. Disrupted functional connectivity within the DMN may underlie difficulties in sustaining attention and maintaining task-related focus observed in ADHD.
3. **Salience Network**: The salience network, responsible for detecting and orienting attention towards salient stimuli, shows altered connectivity patterns in individuals with ADHD. Dysregulated salience network activity may contribute to difficulties in attentional control and response to environmental stimuli characteristic of ADHD.

Neurochemistry

1. **Dopamine Dysregulation**: Dysregulation of dopaminergic neurotransmission, particularly within mesocorticolimbic and nigrostriatal pathways, is implicated in ADHD. Abnormalities in dopamine receptor density, dopamine transporter availability, and dopamine release contribute to deficits in reward processing, inhibitory control, and motor function observed in ADHD.

2. **Noradrenergic Dysfunction**: Alterations in noradrenergic signaling, involving the locus coeruleus-norepinephrine system, are implicated in ADHD. Dysregulated noradrenergic activity contributes to deficits in arousal, attentional control, and behavioral regulation observed in individuals with ADHD.

3. **Serotonergic Modulation**: Serotonergic neurotransmission, mediated by the serotonin transporter and serotonin receptors, also plays a role in ADHD. Dysregulated serotonergic signaling may contribute to emotional dysregulation, impulsivity, and mood instability observed in individuals with ADHD.

Chapter 3: ADHD in Children

Identifying symptoms in young children

Inattention Symptoms

1. **Difficulty Sustaining Attention**: The child may have difficulty focusing on tasks or activities, especially those that require sustained attention, such as listening to stories, completing puzzles, or playing with toys.

2. **Easily Distracted**: The child may become easily distracted by external stimuli or internal thoughts, leading to frequent shifts in attention and difficulty staying on task.

3. **Forgetfulness**: The child may frequently forget instructions, lose belongings, or fail to complete tasks due to forgetfulness or inattention.

4. **Difficulty Organizing Tasks**: The child may struggle with organizing tasks and materials, leading to disorganization, incomplete assignments, and difficulty following routines.
5. **Avoidance of Tasks Requiring Mental Effort**: The child may avoid or procrastinate tasks that require sustained mental effort, such as schoolwork or chores, due to perceived difficulty or frustration.

Hyperactivity Symptoms

1. **Excessive Fidgeting or Squirming**: The child may engage in constant movement, such as tapping hands or feet, squirming in their seat, or shifting positions frequently, even when it is not appropriate.
2. **Difficulty Remaining Seated**: The child may have difficulty staying seated during activities that require sitting still, such as meals, circle time, or quiet play.
3. **Running or Climbing Excessively**: The child may engage in running, climbing, or other physical activities excessively, even in situations where it is unsafe or inappropriate.
4. **Talking Excessively**: The child may talk excessively, interrupting others or dominating conversations without considering social cues or turn-taking.
5. **Difficulty Playing Quietly**: The child may have difficulty engaging in quiet play or activities, preferring active or noisy play.

Impulsivity Symptoms

1. **Blurting Out Answers**: The child may blurt out answers to questions before they have been fully asked, interrupting others or speaking out of turn.

2. **Difficulty Waiting Turn**: The child may have difficulty waiting their turn in games, conversations, or activities, becoming impatient or disruptive.
3. **Interrupting Others**: The child may frequently interrupt or intrude on others' conversations or activities, failing to wait for appropriate opportunities to speak or participate.
4. **Impulsive Decision-Making**: The child may act impulsively without considering consequences, engaging in risky or dangerous behaviors without hesitation.

Other Behavioral Patterns

1. **Temperament and Emotional Regulation**: Children with ADHD may exhibit emotional dysregulation, including frequent mood swings, temper outbursts, or difficulty managing frustration and anger.
2. **Social Difficulties**: The child may struggle with social interactions, having difficulty making and keeping friends, sharing toys, or following social rules.
3. **Academic Challenges**: Children with ADHD may experience difficulties in school, including poor academic performance, incomplete assignments, and disruptive behavior in the classroom.
4. **Sleep Problems**: Some children with ADHD may experience sleep disturbances, including difficulty falling asleep, restless sleep, or frequent nighttime awakenings.

Observation and Evaluation

Identifying ADHD symptoms in young children requires careful observation of behavior across different settings and contexts, including home, school, and social environments. It is essential to consider the frequency, severity, and persistence of symptoms and their impact on the child's daily functioning and well-being.

If you suspect that a young child may have ADHD, it is advisable to consult with a healthcare professional, such as a pediatrician, psychologist, or developmental specialist, for a comprehensive evaluation. A thorough assessment may include clinical interviews, behavior rating scales, developmental screenings, and observations to determine whether the child meets diagnostic criteria for ADHD and to rule out other possible explanations for their behavior. Early intervention and support can help children with ADHD develop coping strategies, improve academic and social skills, and enhance their overall quality of life.

Impact on learning and development

Academic Achievement

1. **Executive Functioning**: ADHD often impairs executive functions such as attention regulation, inhibitory control, working memory, and cognitive flexibility, which are essential for academic success. Children with ADHD may struggle with tasks requiring sustained attention, organization, planning, and problem-solving skills.
2. **Reading and Writing Skills**: ADHD can impact literacy development, including reading comprehension, fluency, and written expression. Difficulties with attention, concentration,

and impulsivity may interfere with decoding, comprehension, and written composition skills.

3. **Mathematics Skills**: Children with ADHD may experience challenges in mathematics, including calculation, problem-solving, and mathematical reasoning. Weaknesses in working memory, attention to detail, and task persistence can hinder mathematical performance and achievement.

4. **Academic Engagement**: ADHD-related symptoms such as inattention, hyperactivity, and impulsivity can affect academic engagement and participation in classroom activities. Children with ADHD may struggle to stay focused, complete assignments, and follow instructions, leading to academic underachievement and disengagement.

Cognitive Functioning

1. **Attentional Control**: ADHD is characterized by difficulties with attention regulation, including maintaining focus, shifting attention, and resisting distractions. Impaired attentional control can impact learning and memory processes, hindering the acquisition and retention of new information.

2. **Working Memory**: Working memory deficits are common in individuals with ADHD, affecting the ability to hold and manipulate information in mind while performing cognitive tasks. Weak working memory skills can impair academic performance, problem-solving abilities, and comprehension of complex information.

3. **Processing Speed**: Children with ADHD may exhibit slower processing speed, characterized by delays in information processing and response time. Reduced processing speed can contribute to difficulties with task completion, time management, and academic productivity.

4. **Cognitive Flexibility**: ADHD often involves deficits in cognitive flexibility, the ability to adapt and shift

strategies in response to changing task demands. Rigidity in thinking and difficulties with task switching can impede problem-solving skills and inhibit academic progress.

Social-Emotional Well-being

1. **Peer Relationships**: Children with ADHD may experience social difficulties, including peer rejection, social isolation, and conflict with peers. Impulsivity, hyperactivity, and inattention can disrupt social interactions, compromise social skills development, and undermine positive peer relationships.
2. **Emotional Regulation**: ADHD is associated with emotional dysregulation, including heightened emotional reactivity, mood instability, and difficulty managing frustration and anger. Emotional dysregulation can exacerbate behavioral problems, impair social functioning, and contribute to psychosocial difficulties.
3. **Self-esteem and Self-concept**: Children with ADHD may struggle with low self-esteem, negative self-perceptions, and feelings of inadequacy. Academic challenges, social rejection, and perceived failure may erode self-confidence and self-efficacy, impacting motivation and academic engagement.
4. **Psychological Well-being**: ADHD is associated with an increased risk of psychological problems, including anxiety, depression, and conduct problems. Co-occurring mental health issues can exacerbate ADHD symptoms, impair functioning across domains, and compromise overall well-being.

Intervention and Support

Effective intervention and support strategies for children with ADHD involve a multi-modal approach targeting academic, cognitive, and socio-emotional domains. This may include:

- **Educational Accommodations**: Providing academic accommodations such as extended time on tests, preferential seating, and modified assignments to address ADHD-related challenges in the classroom.
- **Behavioral Interventions**: Implementing behavioral strategies such as positive reinforcement, behavioral contracts, and token economies to promote self-regulation, task persistence, and academic engagement.
- **Cognitive Remediation**: Offering cognitive training programs targeting executive functions such as working memory, attention, and inhibitory control to enhance cognitive skills and academic performance.
- **Social Skills Training**: Conducting social skills interventions to improve peer relationships, communication skills, and conflict resolution abilities in children with ADHD.
- **Parent and Teacher Training**: Providing parent training programs and teacher professional development workshops to enhance understanding of ADHD, implement effective behavior management strategies, and collaborate on intervention plans.

By addressing the impact of ADHD on learning and development through comprehensive intervention and support, we can empower children with ADHD to achieve academic success, develop essential skills, and thrive in educational and social settings.

Strategies for Parents

1. **Establish Routines**: Create consistent daily routines and schedules for meals, homework, bedtime, and other activities to provide structure and predictability for the child with ADHD.
2. **Set Clear Expectations**: Clearly communicate expectations and rules for behavior, chores, and academic tasks, and provide positive reinforcement for compliance and effort.
3. **Break Tasks into Manageable Steps**: Break down tasks and assignments into smaller, manageable steps, and provide visual or written instructions to help the child stay organized and focused.
4. **Use Visual Aids**: Use visual schedules, checklists, and reminders to help the child with ADHD remember tasks, deadlines, and responsibilities.
5. **Provide Positive Reinforcement**: Offer praise, encouragement, and rewards for positive behaviors, effort, and accomplishments to reinforce desired behaviors and motivate the child.
6. **Encourage Movement and Exercise**: Encourage regular physical activity and movement breaks to help the child with ADHD release excess energy, improve focus, and regulate mood.
7. **Teach Self-regulation Skills**: Teach the child relaxation techniques, mindfulness exercises, and self-calming strategies to manage stress, frustration, and impulsivity.
8. **Limit Distractions**: Create a quiet, organized study space free from distractions such as noise, clutter, and electronic

devices to help the child concentrate on tasks and homework.

9. **Model Organization and Time Management**: Demonstrate and model organizational skills, time management techniques, and problem-solving strategies to help the child develop these essential skills.

10. **Seek Support and Resources**: Seek support from healthcare professionals, educators, and support groups for guidance, information, and resources to help navigate challenges associated with ADHD.

Strategies for Teachers

1. **Provide Clear Instructions**: Give clear, concise instructions and directions, and repeat key information to ensure understanding for students with ADHD.

2. **Use Visual Supports**: Use visual aids, graphic organizers, and visual schedules to help students with ADHD understand and remember information, tasks, and routines.

3. **Break Tasks into Smaller Steps**: Break down assignments and tasks into smaller, manageable steps, and provide step-by-step guidance and support as needed.

4. **Offer Frequent Feedback**: Provide frequent feedback, praise, and encouragement for effort, progress, and improvement to reinforce positive behaviors and motivate students.

5. **Use Active Learning Strategies**: Incorporate active learning strategies, hands-on activities, and movement breaks to engage students with ADHD and accommodate their need for physical activity and stimulation.

6. **Implement Behavior Management Techniques**: Use behavior management techniques such as positive reinforcement, token economies, and behavior contracts to promote appropriate behavior and self-regulation.

7. **Provide Structure and Predictability**: Establish predictable routines, procedures, and classroom expectations to create a structured learning environment that supports students with ADHD.
8. **Encourage Organization Skills**: Teach and reinforce organizational skills such as using planners, keeping track of assignments, and managing materials to help students with ADHD stay organized and on task.
9. **Allow for Movement and Flexible Seating**: Allow students with ADHD to move around the classroom, take movement breaks, and use flexible seating options to accommodate their need for physical activity and sensory input.
10. **Collaborate with Parents**: Maintain open communication with parents and caregivers to share information, exchange feedback, and collaborate on strategies to support the child's academic and behavioral needs.

By implementing these strategies consistently and collaboratively, parents and teachers can create a supportive, structured environment that empowers children with ADHD to succeed academically, develop essential skills, and thrive socially and emotionally.

Chapter 4: ADHD in Adolescents

Challenges unique to teenagers

Academic Challenges

1. **Increased Academic Demands**: Adolescents with ADHD face increased academic demands, including longer assignments,

more complex coursework, and higher expectations for independence and self-management.

2. **Executive Functioning Deficits**: ADHD-related deficits in executive functions such as organization, time management, planning, and self-regulation can impact academic performance, leading to difficulties with homework completion, project management, and test preparation.

3. **Transition to High School**: Transitioning to high school can be particularly challenging for teenagers with ADHD due to the larger, more impersonal environment, increased academic rigor, and greater emphasis on academic achievement and responsibility.

4. **Peer Pressure and Social Dynamics**: Adolescents with ADHD may struggle with social interactions, peer relationships, and navigating social hierarchies, leading to feelings of isolation, rejection, and low self-esteem.

Emotional Regulation

1. **Intense Emotions**: Teenagers with ADHD may experience intense emotions, mood swings, and difficulty regulating their emotions, which can contribute to emotional dysregulation, impulsivity, and risk-taking behaviors.

2. **Identity Formation**: Adolescence is a period of identity formation and self-discovery, during which teenagers with ADHD may struggle with issues of self-esteem, self-concept, and identity development, particularly in the face of academic and social challenges.

3. **Co-occurring Mental Health Issues**: Adolescents with ADHD are at increased risk for co-occurring mental health issues such as anxiety, depression, and substance abuse, which can exacerbate ADHD symptoms and impair functioning across domains.

Risk-taking Behaviors

1. **Impulsivity and Risk-taking**: Adolescents with ADHD may engage in impulsive, risky behaviors such as substance use, reckless driving, unsafe sexual practices, and sensation-seeking activities, placing them at increased risk for accidents, injuries, and negative consequences.
2. **Peer Influence**: Peer pressure and the desire for social acceptance may influence adolescents with ADHD to engage in risky behaviors, leading to impulsivity, poor decision-making, and involvement in delinquent or antisocial activities.

Transition to Adulthood

1. **College and Career Readiness**: Transitioning to adulthood involves preparing for college, vocational training, or employment, which can pose challenges for teenagers with ADHD in terms of academic achievement, career exploration, and independent living skills.
2. **Self-advocacy and Independence**: Adolescents with ADHD need to develop self-advocacy skills, self-awareness, and self-management strategies to advocate for their needs, access support services, and navigate academic and workplace accommodations.
3. **Financial Management**: Managing finances, budgeting, and financial planning are essential skills for adulthood that may be particularly challenging for teenagers with ADHD due to impulsivity, disorganization, and difficulties with planning and decision-making.

Strategies for Support

1. **Education and Awareness**: Educate teenagers with ADHD, their families, and educators about ADHD, its symptoms, and its impact on academic, social, and emotional functioning to promote understanding, empathy, and effective support.
2. **Skill-building and Coping Strategies**: Teach adolescents with ADHD executive functioning skills, time management techniques, organizational strategies, and coping mechanisms to manage academic demands, regulate emotions, and navigate social challenges.
3. **Multimodal Treatment**: Implement a multimodal treatment approach incorporating medication, behavioral interventions, academic accommodations, and psychoeducation to address ADHD symptoms and associated difficulties comprehensively.
4. **Social Skills Training**: Provide social skills training, peer support groups, and opportunities for social interaction and relationship-building to help adolescents with ADHD develop social competence, communication skills, and peer relationships.
5. **Transition Planning**: Develop transition plans and support systems to facilitate the transition to adulthood, including college and career planning, vocational training, independent living skills development, and

access to community resources and support services.

Academic and social implications

Academic Implications

1. **Underachievement**: Adolescents with ADHD may struggle to meet academic expectations, leading to lower grades, incomplete assignments, and academic underachievement compared to their peers.
2. **Difficulty with Executive Functions**: ADHD-related deficits in executive functions such as organization, time management, planning, and self-regulation can impair academic performance, hindering the ability to complete tasks, manage deadlines, and follow instructions.
3. **Inattention and Impulsivity**: Inattention and impulsivity can interfere with learning, concentration, and information processing, making it challenging for adolescents with ADHD to focus on tasks, sustain attention, and retain information.
4. **Procrastination and Disorganization**: Difficulties with task initiation, procrastination, and disorganization can contribute to academic difficulties, resulting in missed deadlines, incomplete assignments, and poor time management skills.
5. **Test-taking Difficulties**: Adolescents with ADHD may struggle with test-taking skills, including difficulties with attention, concentration, and test anxiety, which can impact performance on standardized tests and assessments.

Social Implications

1. **Peer Rejection and Social Isolation**: Adolescents with ADHD may experience peer rejection, social exclusion, and difficulty forming and maintaining friendships due to

social awkwardness, impulsivity, and behavioral differences.

2. **Social Skills Deficits**: ADHD-related impairments in social skills such as communication, empathy, and perspective-taking can hinder social interactions and lead to misunderstandings, conflicts, and peer rejection.

3. **Misinterpretation of Social Cues**: Adolescents with ADHD may misinterpret social cues, signals, and nonverbal communication, leading to social misunderstandings, social faux pas, and difficulty navigating social situations.

4. **Bullying and Victimization**: Adolescents with ADHD are at increased risk for bullying victimization due to social vulnerabilities, impulsivity, and difficulties with peer relationships, which can have negative consequences for self-esteem and emotional well-being.

5. **Loneliness and Low Self-esteem**: Social difficulties and peer rejection can contribute to feelings of loneliness, low self-esteem, and social withdrawal in adolescents with ADHD, exacerbating emotional and psychological distress.

Academic and Social Interventions

1. **Educational Support**: Provide academic accommodations and support services such as extended time on tests, preferential seating, and academic tutoring to address ADHD-related academic difficulties and promote academic success.

2. **Social Skills Training**: Offer social skills training programs, peer support groups, and social competence interventions to help adolescents with ADHD develop social skills, improve communication, and build positive peer relationships.

3. **Behavioral Interventions**: Implement behavioral interventions such as positive reinforcement,

behavior contracts, and social reinforcement to promote appropriate behavior, self-regulation, and social engagement.
4. **Parent and Teacher Collaboration**: Facilitate collaboration between parents, teachers, and mental health professionals to develop individualized intervention plans, share information, and provide consistent support across home and school environments.
5. **Peer Support and Inclusion**: Foster peer support and inclusion through peer mentoring programs, buddy systems, and inclusive classroom practices to promote social acceptance, friendship development, and positive peer relationships.

Managing transitions to adulthood

Academic and Career Planning

1. **Explore Post-secondary Options**: Assist individuals with ADHD in exploring post-secondary education options, including colleges, universities, vocational schools, and training programs, based on their interests, strengths, and career goals.
2. **Access Support Services**: Ensure access to academic support services, disability accommodations, and specialized programs for students with ADHD, such as tutoring, academic coaching, and assistive technology, to facilitate academic success.
3. **Career Exploration and Development**: Provide guidance and resources for career exploration, job shadowing, internships, and volunteer opportunities to help individuals with ADHD identify potential career paths and develop vocational skills and interests.

4. **Transition Planning Meetings**: Conduct transition planning meetings involving the individual, family members, educators, and relevant professionals to develop individualized transition plans outlining academic, vocational, and career goals, as well as support needs and services.

Independent Living Skills Development

1. **Daily Living Skills Training**: Teach practical skills for independent living, such as budgeting, meal planning, grocery shopping, cooking, laundry, transportation, and time management, to foster self-sufficiency and autonomy.
2. **Housing Options**: Explore housing options for individuals with ADHD, including dormitory living, shared housing, independent living arrangements, and supported housing programs, based on their needs, preferences, and abilities.
3. **Self-care and Health Management**: Educate individuals with ADHD about self-care practices, health maintenance, medication management, and coping strategies for managing ADHD symptoms and promoting overall well-being.
4. **Community Resources**: Connect individuals with ADHD to community resources and support services, such as vocational rehabilitation programs, mental health clinics, independent living centers, and peer support groups, to address their needs and promote independence.

Social and Emotional Adjustment

1. **Social Skills Development**: Offer social skills training, peer support groups, and socialization opportunities to help individuals with ADHD develop interpersonal

skills, build friendships, and navigate social situations effectively.

2. **Emotional Regulation Strategies**: Teach coping strategies, relaxation techniques, and stress management skills to help individuals with ADHD regulate emotions, cope with stressors, and maintain psychological well-being during the transition to adulthood.

3. **Self-advocacy and Communication Skills**: Empower individuals with ADHD to advocate for their needs, communicate effectively, and seek support from peers, educators, employers, and service providers as they navigate academic, vocational, and social challenges.

4. **Identity and Self-esteem**: Foster a positive sense of identity, self-esteem, and self-confidence in individuals with ADHD by recognizing their strengths, accomplishments, and unique contributions, and providing encouragement and support for their goals and aspirations.

Accessing Support Services and Resources

1. **Transition Planning Coordination**: Coordinate transition planning efforts and collaborate with relevant stakeholders, including educators, healthcare professionals, vocational counselors, and community agencies, to ensure continuity of care and support across different settings and services.

2. **Information and Referral Services**: Provide information and referral services to help individuals with ADHD and their families access support services, financial assistance,

healthcare resources, and community-based programs available to adults with disabilities.

3. **Advocacy and Legal Rights**: Educate individuals with ADHD about their legal rights, entitlements, and protections under disability rights laws, such as the Americans with Disabilities Act (ADA), and provide advocacy support to help them navigate systems and secure accommodations and services.

4. **Family Support and Education**: Offer family support services, counseling, and educational resources to help families of individuals with ADHD understand the transition process, navigate challenges, and advocate for their loved one's needs effectively.

Chapter 5: ADHD in Adults

Recognizing ADHD in adult life

Inattention Symptoms

1. **Difficulty Concentrating**: Adults with ADHD may have difficulty focusing on tasks, sustaining attention, and maintaining productivity, particularly in activities that are repetitive, boring, or unstimulating.
2. **Disorganization**: Chronic disorganization, forgetfulness, and difficulties with time management and prioritization are common features of ADHD in adults, leading to missed appointments, procrastination, and difficulty meeting deadlines.
3. **Forgetfulness**: Adults with ADHD may frequently forget important dates, appointments, and obligations, as well as

misplace items and belongings due to lapses in memory and attention.

4. **Easily Distracted**: Adults with ADHD may be easily distracted by external stimuli, interruptions, and irrelevant thoughts, leading to difficulty staying on task and completing assignments or projects.

5. **Poor Attention to Detail**: Adults with ADHD may struggle with attention to detail, making careless mistakes, overlooking important information, and failing to follow through on instructions or tasks.

Hyperactivity Symptoms

1. **Restlessness**: While hyperactivity tends to decrease with age, adults with ADHD may still experience inner restlessness, fidgeting, and a need for constant movement or stimulation, particularly in situations that require prolonged sitting or concentration.

2. **Impulsivity**: Impulsive behaviors such as interrupting others, blurting out responses, and making impulsive decisions without considering consequences are common features of ADHD in adults, contributing to difficulties in social and professional interactions.

3. **Excessive Talking**: Adults with ADHD may engage in excessive talking, interrupting conversations, and difficulty waiting their turn in social situations, leading to communication difficulties and social awkwardness.

Emotional Dysregulation

1. **Mood Swings**: Emotional dysregulation, including mood swings, irritability, and emotional sensitivity, is common in adults with ADHD, contributing to

difficulties in interpersonal relationships and coping with stressors.
2. **Rejection Sensitivity**: Adults with ADHD may be particularly sensitive to criticism, rejection, and negative feedback, leading to feelings of insecurity, low self-esteem, and social anxiety.
3. **Impulsivity in Emotions**: Adults with ADHD may struggle with impulse control in emotional reactions, reacting impulsively to perceived slights or frustrations, and experiencing difficulty calming down or regulating emotions.

Behavioral Patterns

1. **Procrastination**: Chronic procrastination, avoidance of tasks, and difficulty initiating and completing projects are common behavioral patterns in adults with ADHD, leading to challenges in academic, professional, and personal domains.
2. **Difficulty with Planning and Organization**: Adults with ADHD may struggle with planning, organizing, and prioritizing tasks, leading to difficulties in managing time, meeting deadlines, and achieving long-term goals.
3. **Risk-taking Behaviors**: Impulsivity and sensation-seeking tendencies may lead adults with ADHD to engage in risky behaviors such as reckless driving, substance abuse, and gambling, increasing their vulnerability to accidents, injuries, and negative consequences.

Impact on Daily Functioning

1. **Academic and Occupational Impairment**: ADHD can significantly impair academic and occupational functioning in adults, leading to difficulties in employment, job performance, and career advancement.
2. **Interpersonal Difficulties**: Adults with ADHD may experience challenges in interpersonal relationships, including conflicts, misunderstandings, and social isolation, due to difficulties with communication, emotional regulation, and social skills.
3. **Self-esteem and Mental Health**: ADHD is associated with increased risk of co-occurring mental health issues such as anxiety, depression, and substance abuse, which can further exacerbate symptoms and impair overall functioning and well-being.

Seeking Diagnosis and Treatment

If you suspect that you or someone you know may have ADHD in adulthood, it is important to seek evaluation and diagnosis from a qualified healthcare professional, such as a psychiatrist, psychologist, or primary care physician, who specializes in ADHD assessment and treatment. A comprehensive evaluation may include clinical interviews, self-report questionnaires, behavioral assessments, and review of medical history to assess symptoms, impairments, and functional difficulties associated with ADHD.

Once diagnosed, treatment options for ADHD in adults may include medication, psychotherapy, cognitive-behavioral therapy (CBT), coaching, and lifestyle modifications to address symptoms, improve coping skills, and enhance overall functioning and quality of life. By recognizing and addressing ADHD in adulthood, individuals can access the support and resources needed to manage their symptoms effectively, achieve their goals, and thrive in personal and professional life.

3.5

Workplace challenges and accommodations

Workplace Challenges:

1. **Difficulty Concentrating**: Individuals with ADHD may struggle to maintain focus and attention on tasks, leading to distractions, errors, and difficulty completing assignments.
2. **Disorganization**: Chronic disorganization and difficulty with time management may result in missed deadlines, forgotten appointments, and difficulty prioritizing tasks.
3. **Procrastination**: Procrastination and difficulty initiating tasks can lead to last-minute rushes, increased stress, and lower-quality work.
4. **Impulsivity**: Impulsive behaviors such as interrupting others, blurting out responses, and making impulsive decisions can disrupt meetings, communication, and teamwork.
5. **Overwhelm**: Overstimulation, multitasking, and information overload may overwhelm individuals with ADHD, leading to stress, anxiety, and difficulty processing information.

Accommodations and Strategies:

1. **Structured Environment**: Provide a structured work environment with clear expectations, routines, and deadlines to help individuals with ADHD stay organized and focused.
2. **Task Lists and Reminders**: Encourage the use of task lists, calendars, and reminders to help individuals with ADHD manage their workload, prioritize tasks, and meet deadlines.
3. **Break Tasks into Smaller Steps**: Break down complex tasks into smaller, manageable steps, and provide clear instructions and guidance to help individuals with ADHD stay on track.
4. **Time Management Tools**: Offer time management tools such as timers, alarms, and scheduling apps to help individuals with ADHD manage their time effectively and pace themselves throughout the day.
5. **Flexible Work Arrangements**: Consider flexible work arrangements such as telecommuting, flexible hours, and alternative workspaces to accommodate the individual needs and preferences of employees with ADHD.
6. **Quiet Workspaces**: Provide quiet, distraction-free workspaces or accommodations such as noise-cancelling headphones to minimize distractions and support concentration for individuals with ADHD.
7. **Regular Check-ins and Feedback**: Schedule regular check-ins and provide constructive feedback to help individuals with ADHD stay on track, monitor progress, and adjust strategies as needed.
8. **Training and Skill Development**: Offer training programs, workshops, and coaching to help individuals with ADHD develop essential skills such as time management, organization, and communication in the workplace.

9. **Supportive Workplace Culture**: Foster a supportive and inclusive workplace culture that promotes understanding, empathy, and accommodation for individuals with ADHD, and encourages open communication and collaboration among team members.
10. **Employee Assistance Programs (EAP)**: Provide access to employee assistance programs offering counseling, coaching, and resources to support employees with ADHD in managing stress, coping with challenges, and balancing work and personal life.

Relationships and family life

Impact on Relationships:

1. **Communication Challenges**: ADHD-related difficulties with attention, impulsivity, and organization can hinder effective communication in relationships, leading to misunderstandings, conflicts, and frustration.
2. **Emotional Dysregulation**: Emotional dysregulation, mood swings, and impulsivity associated with ADHD can strain relationships, causing tension, arguments, and emotional volatility.
3. **Forgetfulness and Disorganization**: Forgetfulness, disorganization, and difficulty following through on commitments may lead to feelings of neglect, frustration, and resentment in partners and family members.
4. **Time Management Issues**: ADHD-related difficulties with time management and prioritization can disrupt schedules, appointments, and family routines, causing stress and conflicts over responsibilities.
5. **Impulsivity and Risk-taking**: Impulsivity and risk-taking behaviors associated with ADHD may lead to impulsive

decisions, financial difficulties, and reckless behaviors that strain relationships and undermine trust.

Strategies for Managing Relationships:

1. **Education and Awareness**: Educate yourself and your partner or family members about ADHD, its symptoms, and its impact on relationships to promote understanding, empathy, and effective communication.
2. **Open Communication**: Foster open and honest communication in relationships, allowing partners and family members to express their needs, concerns, and feelings in a supportive and non-judgmental environment.
3. **Establishing Routines**: Create structured routines and schedules for daily activities, household tasks, and family responsibilities to help manage ADHD-related challenges with time management and organization.
4. **Active Listening**: Practice active listening and empathy in relationships, seeking to understand each other's perspectives, feelings, and needs without judgment or criticism.
5. **Problem-solving Skills**: Develop problem-solving skills and conflict resolution strategies to address issues and disagreements constructively, working together as a team to find mutually acceptable solutions.
6. **Seeking Support**: Seek support from mental health professionals, support groups, or couples therapy to address relationship challenges related to ADHD and develop coping strategies and communication skills.

Impact on Family Life:

1. **Parenting Challenges**: Parenting a child with ADHD can be particularly challenging due to the demands of managing ADHD-related behaviors, academic difficulties, and emotional regulation issues.
2. **Family Dynamics**: ADHD can disrupt family dynamics and relationships, affecting sibling relationships, parental roles, and overall family cohesion.
3. **Financial Strain**: Financial difficulties resulting from impulsivity, job instability, or treatment costs can create stress and strain on family relationships and household finances.
4. **Emotional Toll**: Managing the emotional toll of ADHD on family life, including feelings of frustration, guilt, and exhaustion, can impact the well-being and mental health of all family members.

Strategies for Managing Family Life:

1. **Parent Education and Support**: Seek parent education and support programs, therapy, or support groups to learn effective parenting strategies, coping skills, and stress management techniques for managing ADHD in children.
2. **Family Therapy**: Consider family therapy or counseling to address family dynamics, improve communication, and strengthen relationships among family members impacted by ADHD.
3. **Shared Responsibilities**: Distribute household responsibilities and parenting tasks equitably among family members to reduce stress and support each other in managing the challenges of ADHD.

4. **Self-care**: Prioritize self-care and well-being for yourself and other family members, including setting aside time for relaxation, hobbies, and activities that promote mental and emotional health.
5. **Celebrate Successes**: Celebrate small victories and successes as a family, acknowledging progress, effort, and resilience in managing ADHD-related challenges together.

Chapter 06: ADHD and Executive Functioning

How ADHD affects planning, organization, and time management

Planning:

1. **Difficulty Setting Goals**: Individuals with ADHD may have difficulty setting and prioritizing goals, leading to uncertainty about where to start and how to allocate time and resources effectively.
2. **Impaired Future Thinking**: ADHD can impair the ability to think ahead and anticipate future consequences, making it challenging to plan and prepare for upcoming events, tasks, or projects.
3. **Lack of Strategic Thinking**: Individuals with ADHD may struggle to develop and implement effective strategies for achieving goals, leading to haphazard or inefficient approaches to problem-solving and decision-making.
4. **Poor Long-term Planning**: ADHD-related impulsivity and short-term thinking may result in a lack of consideration for long-term consequences or future outcomes, leading to procrastination and difficulty with long-term planning.

Organization:

1. **Chronic Disorganization**: Individuals with ADHD often struggle with organization and maintaining order in their physical environment, leading to clutter, messiness, and difficulty locating items or information when needed.
2. **Difficulty with Task Sequencing**: Sequencing tasks in a logical order and prioritizing activities can be challenging for individuals with ADHD, resulting in a lack of structure and coherence in their approach to tasks and projects.
3. **Ineffective Time Management**: Poor time management skills, such as underestimating the time needed to complete tasks or failing to allocate time appropriately, contribute to disorganization and difficulty meeting deadlines.
4. **Forgetfulness**: ADHD-related forgetfulness and absentmindedness may result in missed appointments, forgotten deadlines, and incomplete tasks, undermining efforts to stay organized and on track.

Time Management:

1. **Procrastination**: Procrastination is a common issue for individuals with ADHD, who may delay starting tasks or projects due to difficulty with task initiation, motivation, and time estimation.
2. **Difficulty Estimating Time**: ADHD can impair the ability to accurately estimate the time needed to complete tasks, leading to overcommitment, unrealistic expectations, and frustration when tasks take longer than anticipated.
3. **Time Blindness**: Individuals with ADHD may experience "time blindness," a sense of time passing inconsistently or unpredictably, making it

challenging to manage time effectively and adhere to schedules or deadlines.
4. **Impulsivity in Time Management**: Impulsive behaviors and distractions can disrupt time management efforts, leading to time-consuming tangents, interruptions, and difficulty staying focused on tasks or priorities.

Strategies for Addressing Challenges:

1. **Break Tasks into Smaller Steps**: Break down tasks and projects into smaller, manageable steps to reduce overwhelm and facilitate planning and organization.
2. **Use Visual Aids**: Utilize visual aids such as calendars, planners, checklists, and reminders to help organize tasks, set goals, and track progress.
3. **Set Clear Priorities**: Identify and prioritize tasks based on importance and urgency, focusing on high-priority tasks first and allocating time and resources accordingly.
4. **Establish Routines**: Create structured routines and daily schedules to provide consistency and predictability, helping individuals with ADHD stay organized and manage their time effectively.
5. **Practice Time Management Techniques**: Teach and practice time management techniques such as setting timers, using time-blocking techniques, and breaking tasks into timed intervals to improve time awareness and task efficiency.
6. **Seek Support and Accountability**: Enlist the support of family members, friends, or

colleagues to provide accountability, encouragement, and assistance with planning, organization, and time management.

7. **Professional Help**: Consider seeking assistance from mental health professionals, coaches, or organizational specialists who specialize in ADHD to develop personalized strategies and interventions for improving planning, organization, and time management skills.

Individualized Education Programs (IEPs)

Components of an IEP:

1. **Present Level of Performance (PLOP)**: The IEP begins with a description of the student's current academic, functional, and developmental levels, including strengths, weaknesses, and areas of need related to ADHD.
2. **Annual Goals and Objectives**: Based on the student's PLOP, the IEP team develops measurable annual goals and objectives in areas such as academic achievement, functional skills, social-emotional development, and behavior management.
3. **Special Education Services and Supports**: The IEP specifies the specialized instruction, accommodations, modifications, and support services needed to help the student achieve their annual goals and access the general education curriculum.
4. **Related Services**: If deemed necessary, the IEP may include related services such as occupational therapy, speech-language therapy, counseling, or behavioral intervention services to address specific needs related to ADHD.
5. **Accommodations and Modifications**: The IEP outlines accommodations and modifications tailored to the student's needs, such as extended time on tests, preferential seating,

frequent breaks, or assistive technology devices, to support their learning and participation in the classroom.

6. **Transition Planning (for older students)**: For students approaching transition age (typically around age 14 or older), the IEP includes transition planning goals and services to help prepare the student for post-secondary education, vocational training, employment, and independent living.

7. **Parental Involvement and Consent**: Parents or guardians play a central role in the development and review of the IEP, providing input, feedback, and consent for the proposed goals, services, and accommodations outlined in the plan.

Process of Developing an IEP:

1. **Referral and Evaluation**: The process begins with a referral for special education services, followed by a comprehensive evaluation to assess the student's strengths, weaknesses, and eligibility for special education and related services under the Individuals with Disabilities Education Act (IDEA).

2. **IEP Team Meeting**: A multidisciplinary team, including parents or guardians, educators, special education professionals, and relevant specialists, convenes to review evaluation results, develop the IEP, and determine appropriate goals, services, and accommodations for the student.

3. **Annual Review and Revision**: The IEP is reviewed and updated annually to reflect the student's progress, changing needs, and goals for the upcoming year, with input from the IEP team and parental consent for any revisions or modifications to the plan.

4. **Implementation and Monitoring**: Once the IEP is finalized, it is implemented in the classroom setting, with ongoing monitoring and progress monitoring to assess the student's response to interventions, adjust strategies as

needed, and ensure that the student is making meaningful progress towards their goals.

Key Considerations for ADHD:

1. **Executive Functioning Support**: IEP goals and accommodations may focus on developing executive functioning skills such as organization, time management, planning, and self-regulation, which are commonly impacted by ADHD.
2. **Behavior Management Strategies**: The IEP may include behavior management strategies and supports to address ADHD-related challenges such as impulsivity, hyperactivity, and inattention, promoting positive behavior and social-emotional development.
3. **Environmental Supports**: Classroom accommodations and modifications, such as structured routines, visual schedules, and sensory supports, can help create a supportive learning environment that minimizes distractions and supports the student's attention and engagement.
4. **Collaboration and Communication**: Effective collaboration and communication between parents, educators, and other members of the IEP team are essential for ensuring that the student's needs are identified, addressed, and monitored effectively over time.

1. Clear and Consistent Expectations:

- **Establish Routines**: Create predictable routines and schedules for daily activities, transitions, and classroom procedures to provide structure and minimize anxiety for students with ADHD.
- **Set Clear Expectations**: Clearly communicate academic and behavioral expectations, rules, and procedures, and reinforce them consistently to help students understand what is expected of them.

2. Active Engagement and Participation:

- **Interactive Instruction**: Use interactive teaching methods such as hands-on activities, group discussions, and cooperative learning to actively engage students with ADHD and promote active participation in the learning process.
- **Movement Breaks**: Incorporate movement breaks, brain breaks, and physical activities into the lesson to help students with ADHD release excess energy, improve focus, and regulate attention.

3. Multisensory Learning:

- **Multimodal Instruction**: Present information using a variety of sensory modalities (visual, auditory, kinesthetic) to appeal to different learning styles and reinforce learning for students with ADHD.

- **Visual Supports**: Use visual aids such as graphic organizers, charts, diagrams, and visual schedules to enhance comprehension, organization, and memory retention for students with ADHD.

4. Chunking and Scaffolded Instruction:

- **Chunking Information**: Break down complex tasks and instructions into smaller, more manageable chunks to reduce overwhelm and facilitate understanding for students with ADHD.
- **Scaffolded Instruction**: Provide scaffolding and support as needed to help students with ADHD build on their existing skills and gradually work towards independence in completing tasks and assignments.

5. Positive Reinforcement and Feedback:

- **Positive Reinforcement**: Use positive reinforcement, praise, and rewards to acknowledge and reinforce desired behaviors, effort, and academic progress for students with ADHD.
- **Constructive Feedback**: Provide constructive feedback that is specific, timely, and actionable to help students with ADHD understand their strengths and areas for improvement and make necessary adjustments.

6. Executive Functioning Support:

- **Organization Tools**: Teach organizational strategies such as using planners, checklists, color-coding, and digital tools to help students with ADHD manage their time, assignments, and materials effectively.
- **Time Management Skills**: Teach time management skills such as prioritizing tasks, estimating time needed for activities, and breaking tasks into manageable steps to help students with ADHD manage their time more efficiently.

7. Flexible Seating and Environment:

- **Flexible Seating Options**: Provide flexible seating options such as standing desks, stability balls, or fidget tools to accommodate the sensory needs and preferences of students with ADHD and promote focus and engagement.
- **Minimize Distractions**: Create a low-distraction environment by minimizing visual and auditory distractions, seating students away from distractions, and providing quiet spaces for focused work when needed.

8. Individualized Support:

- **Individualized Instruction**: Differentiate instruction and assignments to meet the individual learning needs, interests, and strengths of students with ADHD, providing opportunities for choice and autonomy whenever possible.
- **Collaboration with Support Services**: Work collaboratively with special education professionals,

counselors, and other support personnel to develop and implement individualized support plans (e.g., IEPs, 504 plans) for students with ADHD.

Parent training programs

Key Components:

1. **Education about ADHD**: Parent training programs often begin by providing parents with information about ADHD, its symptoms, causes, and impact on children's behavior, learning, and social-emotional development.
2. **Behavior Management Strategies**: Parents learn evidence-based techniques for managing ADHD-related behaviors, such as setting clear expectations, using positive reinforcement, implementing consistent consequences, and promoting self-regulation skills.
3. **Effective Communication Skills**: Parents acquire communication strategies to improve parent-child communication, active listening, and problem-solving skills, fostering positive interactions and reducing conflict within the family.
4. **Parenting Skills Training**: Parent training programs teach parenting skills such as effective discipline techniques, stress management, and self-care practices to help parents cope with the challenges of raising a child with ADHD.
5. **Collaboration with Schools and Professionals**: Parents learn how to collaborate effectively with teachers, school personnel, and mental health professionals to advocate for their child's needs, access appropriate support services, and promote consistency between home and school environments.
6. **Promotion of Positive Parenting Practices**: Parent training programs emphasize the importance of fostering a supportive, nurturing, and positive parenting environment

that promotes children's self-esteem, resilience, and overall well-being.

Benefits:

1. **Improved Parent-Child Relationships**: Parent training programs help parents build stronger, more positive relationships with their children by enhancing communication, understanding, and empathy for their child's needs and challenges.
2. **Reduced Behavior Problems**: By learning effective behavior management strategies, parents can reduce ADHD-related behavior problems such as impulsivity, hyperactivity, inattention, and defiance, improving family functioning and harmony.
3. **Enhanced Parenting Skills**: Parent training programs equip parents with practical skills and strategies for addressing the unique challenges of parenting a child with ADHD, increasing confidence and competence in their parenting role.
4. **Better Academic and Social Outcomes**: Children of parents who participate in parent training programs for ADHD may experience improved academic performance, social skills, and self-regulation abilities, leading to better overall outcomes in school and social settings.
5. **Decreased Parental Stress**: By providing parents with tools and support for managing ADHD-related challenges, parent training programs can reduce parental stress, frustration, and feelings of helplessness, promoting greater well-being and resilience.
6. **Long-Term Benefits for Children**: Research suggests that parent training programs for ADHD can have lasting benefits for children, with improvements in behavior, academic functioning, and social-emotional development persisting over time.

Chapter 07: Medication for ADHD

Types of medications (stimulants and non-stimulants)

Stimulant Medications:

Stimulant medications are the most commonly prescribed and well-established treatment for ADHD. They work by increasing levels of certain neurotransmitters in the brain, specifically dopamine and norepinephrine, which play a key role in regulating attention, focus, and impulse control. Stimulant medications are available in immediate-release (short-acting) and extended-release (long-acting) formulations.

1. **Methylphenidate-Based Medications**:
   o **Ritalin**: Immediate-release methylphenidate.
   o **Concerta**: Extended-release methylphenidate.
   o **Focalin**: Immediate-release dexmethylphenidate (a more potent form of methylphenidate).
   o **Daytrana**: Methylphenidate patch that provides extended-release delivery.
2. **Amphetamine-Based Medications**:
   o **Adderall**: Immediate-release amphetamine mixed salts.
   o **Adderall XR**: Extended-release amphetamine mixed salts.
   o **Vyvanse**: Prodrug of dextroamphetamine that is metabolized into its active form, providing a long duration of action.

Non-Stimulant Medications:

Non-stimulant medications are alternative options for individuals who do not respond well to or cannot tolerate stimulant medications. They work through different mechanisms of action than stimulants and may have different side effect profiles. Non-stimulant medications are often considered for individuals with certain medical conditions, history of substance abuse, or specific treatment preferences.

1. **Atomoxetine (Strattera)**: Atomoxetine is a selective norepinephrine reuptake inhibitor (SNRI) that increases levels of norepinephrine in the brain. It is approved for the treatment of ADHD in children, adolescents, and adults. Atomoxetine is available in both immediate-release and extended-release formulations.
2. **Guanfacine (Intuniv)** and **Clonidine (Kapvay)**: These medications are alpha-2 adrenergic agonists that affect certain receptors in the brain involved in attention regulation. They are typically used as adjunctive treatments for ADHD or as alternatives for individuals who cannot tolerate stimulant medications. Guanfacine is available in extended-release formulation, while clonidine is available in immediate-release and extended-release formulations.

Choosing the Right Medication:

The choice of medication for ADHD depends on various factors, including individual symptom presentation, medical history, potential side effects, treatment preferences, and response to previous medications. It is important for individuals with ADHD to work closely with a healthcare provider, such as a psychiatrist or pediatrician, to determine the most appropriate medication and dosage based on their specific needs and circumstances. Additionally, ongoing monitoring and adjustment of medication may be necessary to optimize treatment outcomes and minimize side effects.

Benefits:

Stimulant Medications:

1. **Improvement in ADHD Symptoms**: Stimulant medications have been shown to effectively reduce symptoms of inattention, hyperactivity, and impulsivity in many individuals with ADHD, leading to improved focus, attention, and impulse control.
2. **Quick Onset of Action**: Stimulant medications typically start working quickly, often within 30 to 60 minutes after ingestion, providing rapid relief of symptoms.
3. **Long Duration of Action (Extended-Release Formulations)**: Extended-release formulations of stimulant medications offer prolonged symptom control throughout the day, allowing for once-daily dosing and avoiding the need for multiple doses.
4. **Consistent Efficacy**: Stimulant medications maintain their effectiveness over time, with sustained improvement in ADHD symptoms observed with continued use.

Non-Stimulant Medications:

1. **Alternative for Individuals Unresponsive to or Unable to Tolerate Stimulants**: Non-stimulant medications such as atomoxetine, guanfacine, and clonidine offer alternative treatment options for individuals who do not respond well to or cannot tolerate stimulant medications.
2. **Reduced Risk of Abuse or Dependence**: Non-stimulant medications have a lower risk of abuse or dependence compared to stimulant medications, making them

suitable options for individuals with a history of substance abuse or concerns about medication misuse.

3. **Non-Disruptive Sleep Patterns**: Some non-stimulant medications, such as atomoxetine, do not typically disrupt sleep patterns and may be preferred for individuals who experience insomnia or sleep disturbances with stimulant medications.

Potential Side Effects:

Stimulant Medications:

1. **Insomnia**: Stimulant medications can interfere with sleep, leading to difficulty falling asleep or staying asleep, especially if taken later in the day.
2. **Appetite Suppression and Weight Loss**: Stimulant medications may decrease appetite and lead to weight loss, particularly during the initial weeks of treatment.
3. **Growth Suppression (in Children)**: Long-term use of stimulant medications may be associated with a slight decrease in growth rate in children, although catch-up growth typically occurs after discontinuation of treatment.
4. **Cardiovascular Effects**: Stimulant medications may increase heart rate and blood pressure, posing risks for individuals with pre-existing cardiovascular conditions.

Non-Stimulant Medications:

1. **Gastrointestinal Upset**: Non-stimulant medications such as atomoxetine may cause

gastrointestinal side effects such as nausea, vomiting, or stomach pain in some individuals.

2. **Fatigue or Sedation**: Alpha-2 adrenergic agonists like guanfacine and clonidine may cause fatigue, drowsiness, or sedation, particularly when starting or adjusting the dose.

3. **Hypotension (Low Blood Pressure)**: Guanfacine and clonidine may lower blood pressure, leading to symptoms such as dizziness, lightheadedness, or fainting, especially when standing up quickly.

4. **Mood Changes**: Some individuals may experience mood changes, irritability, or emotional lability as side effects of non-stimulant medications, although these effects are typically less common compared to stimulant medications.

Individualized Treatment:

The benefits and potential side effects of ADHD medications vary from person to person, and it's essential for healthcare providers to consider individual factors such as age, medical history, co-existing conditions, and treatment preferences when selecting and monitoring medications. Regular communication between patients, caregivers, and healthcare providers is crucial for optimizing treatment outcomes, managing side effects, and ensuring that the benefits of medication outweigh any potential risks. Additionally, non-pharmacological interventions such as behavioral therapy, education, and support should be integrated into comprehensive treatment plans for ADHD to address the holistic needs of individuals with the disorder.

3.5

Considerations for long-term medication use

1. Monitoring and Assessment:

1. **Regular Follow-Up Visits**: It's essential for individuals on long-term medication to have regular follow-up visits with their healthcare provider to monitor treatment response, adjust medication dosage if needed, and address any emerging concerns or side effects.
2. **Assessment of Symptoms**: Ongoing assessment of ADHD symptoms and functional impairments is crucial to evaluate the effectiveness of medication and make informed decisions about treatment adjustments or modifications.
3. **Monitoring Growth and Development (in Children)**: For children and adolescents, regular monitoring of growth, weight, and developmental milestones is necessary to assess the potential impact of medication on growth rate and ensure appropriate growth trajectory.

2. Safety and Tolerability:

1. **Side Effect Monitoring**: Healthcare providers should monitor for potential side effects associated with long-term medication use, such as insomnia, appetite suppression, weight loss, cardiovascular effects, or mood changes, and address them promptly.
2. **Cardiovascular Risk Assessment**: Individuals on stimulant medications should undergo periodic cardiovascular risk assessment, including monitoring of heart rate, blood pressure, and cardiovascular health, especially if they have pre-existing cardiovascular conditions or risk factors.
3. **Assessment of Abuse Potential**: Healthcare providers should assess the risk of medication misuse, diversion, or

abuse, particularly in individuals with a history of substance abuse or addictive behaviors.

3. Treatment Adherence:

1. **Adherence Monitoring**: Ensuring consistent adherence to medication treatment is essential for maximizing therapeutic benefits and maintaining symptom control over the long term. Strategies to promote adherence may include medication reminders, pill organizers, or behavioral interventions.
2. **Addressing Barriers to Adherence**: Healthcare providers should address any barriers to medication adherence, such as concerns about side effects, forgetfulness, stigma, or difficulty accessing medication, and provide support and resources to overcome these barriers.

4. Individualized Treatment:

1. **Personalized Treatment Plans**: Treatment plans should be individualized based on the unique needs, preferences, and characteristics of each individual with ADHD, taking into account factors such as age, co-existing conditions, treatment response, and lifestyle factors.
2. **Multimodal Treatment Approach**: Long-term management of ADHD often requires a multimodal treatment approach that combines medication with non-pharmacological interventions such as behavioral therapy, education, environmental modifications, and support services.

5. Periodic Reassessment and Review:

1. **Reassessment of Treatment Goals**: Periodic reassessment of treatment goals, priorities, and preferences is necessary to ensure that medication treatment aligns with the individual's evolving needs and goals over time.
2. **Review of Treatment Plan**: Healthcare providers should regularly review the overall treatment plan, including medication regimen, dosage, and adjunctive interventions, to optimize treatment outcomes, address emerging challenges, and make necessary adjustments.

6. Informed Decision-Making:

1. **Shared Decision-Making**: Encouraging shared decision-making between patients, caregivers, and healthcare providers promotes collaborative decision-making, informed consent, and patient-centered care, ensuring that treatment decisions align with the individual's values, preferences, and goals.
2. **Education and Empowerment**: Providing education and information about ADHD, treatment options, potential benefits, and risks empowers individuals and caregivers to make informed decisions about long-term medication use and actively participate in their treatment journey.

Chapter 08: Psychological Therapies

Cognitive Behavioral Therapy (CBT)

Principles of CBT:

1. **Cognitive Restructuring**: CBT helps individuals identify and challenge negative or distorted thought patterns, such as self-criticism, catastrophic thinking, or irrational beliefs, and replace them with more realistic and adaptive thoughts.
2. **Behavioral Activation**: CBT encourages individuals to engage in enjoyable or meaningful activities that promote positive emotions and reduce avoidance or withdrawal behaviors associated with ADHD symptoms.
3. **Skill Building**: CBT teaches practical coping skills and strategies to manage ADHD symptoms, such as time management, organization, problem-solving, assertiveness, and stress management techniques.
4. **Exposure and Response Prevention**: In cases where avoidance behaviors or anxiety-related symptoms are present, CBT may involve gradual exposure to feared or challenging situations and learning alternative responses to reduce anxiety and improve coping.
5. **Homework Assignments**: CBT often includes homework assignments or exercises that reinforce skills learned in therapy sessions, promote self-awareness, and encourage practice of new coping strategies in real-life situations.

Application in ADHD Treatment:

1. **Symptom Management**: CBT helps individuals with ADHD understand their symptoms, triggers, and challenges, and develop effective strategies for managing

inattention, impulsivity, and hyperactivity in various domains of life, such as school, work, and relationships.

2. **Executive Functioning Skills**: CBT targets executive functioning deficits commonly associated with ADHD, such as poor organization, time management, planning, and decision-making skills, by teaching practical techniques for improving these areas.

3. **Emotional Regulation**: CBT helps individuals with ADHD recognize and regulate their emotions, reduce emotional reactivity, and develop healthy coping mechanisms for dealing with frustration, stress, and impulsivity.

4. **Problem-Solving Skills**: CBT teaches problem-solving skills to help individuals with ADHD identify barriers, set achievable goals, generate solutions, and implement action plans to address challenges in various life domains.

5. **Behavioral Interventions**: CBT incorporates behavioral strategies, such as reinforcement techniques, behavioral contracts, and self-monitoring, to promote positive behavior change and reinforce adaptive coping skills.

Effectiveness and Benefits:

1. **Evidence-Based**: CBT for ADHD has been supported by numerous research studies and meta-analyses, demonstrating its effectiveness in reducing ADHD symptoms, improving executive functioning, and enhancing overall functioning and quality of life.

2. **Long-Term Benefits**: CBT has shown sustained benefits over time, with improvements in ADHD symptoms, functional impairment, and psychosocial outcomes observed even after treatment completion.

3. **Complementary Treatment**: CBT can be used alone or in combination with medication management,

educational interventions, and other psychosocial treatments to provide comprehensive and holistic care for individuals with ADHD.

4. **Generalizability**: The skills learned in CBT can be generalized to various life situations and contexts, empowering individuals with ADHD to apply their coping strategies and problem-solving skills across different domains of functioning.

Considerations:

1. **Individualized Treatment**: CBT should be tailored to the unique needs, strengths, and challenges of each individual with ADHD, taking into account factors such as age, symptom severity, co-existing conditions, and treatment preferences.
2. **Collaborative Approach**: Successful implementation of CBT for ADHD often involves collaboration between the individual, therapist, caregivers, and other relevant stakeholders to support treatment adherence, generalization of skills, and maintenance of gains over time.
3. **Treatment Adherence**: Regular attendance and active participation in CBT sessions are essential for maximizing treatment outcomes and achieving lasting benefits, emphasizing the importance of engagement and motivation in the therapeutic process.

Overall, Cognitive Behavioral Therapy (CBT) is a valuable and effective treatment approach for individuals with ADHD, offering practical strategies and skills to manage symptoms, improve functioning, and enhance overall well-being. Through collaborative and individualized treatment, CBT empowers individuals with ADHD to build resilience, overcome challenges, and thrive in various aspects of their lives.

1. Attentional Control:

1. **Enhanced Attention Regulation**: Mindfulness practices, such as focused attention on the breath or body sensations, can strengthen attentional control and improve sustained attention, helping individuals with ADHD stay focused and present in the moment.
2. **Reduced Mind Wandering**: Mindfulness training teaches individuals to notice and redirect attention when it wanders, reducing distractibility and increasing the ability to sustain attention on tasks and activities.

2. Emotional Regulation:

1. **Increased Emotional Awareness**: Mindfulness practices encourage individuals to observe and acknowledge their emotions without judgment, leading to greater emotional awareness and self-understanding, which can be particularly beneficial for individuals with ADHD who may experience emotional dysregulation.
2. **Improved Stress Management**: Mindfulness-based stress reduction techniques help individuals with ADHD develop coping skills for managing stress, anxiety, and overwhelm, reducing the impact of emotional reactivity on daily functioning.

3. Impulse Control:

1. **Greater Impulse Awareness**: Mindfulness practices cultivate awareness of impulses and automatic reactions, allowing individuals with ADHD to pause, reflect, and choose more adaptive responses instead of acting impulsively.
2. **Increased Response Inhibition**: Mindfulness training strengthens the capacity for response inhibition, the ability to control impulsive behaviors and delay gratification, which is often impaired in individuals with ADHD.

4. Executive Functioning:

1. **Improved Working Memory**: Mindfulness practices can enhance working memory capacity and efficiency, supporting cognitive processes involved in planning, problem-solving, and decision-making, which are commonly affected in individuals with ADHD.
2. **Enhanced Self-Regulation Skills**: Mindfulness training promotes self-regulation skills such as goal-setting, self-monitoring, and self-control, facilitating better executive functioning and adaptive behavior in various life domains.

5. Overall Well-Being:

1. **Stress Reduction and Relaxation**: Mindfulness techniques, such as mindful breathing or body scan exercises, promote relaxation, reduce physiological arousal,

and alleviate symptoms of anxiety and stress commonly experienced by individuals with ADHD.

2. **Increased Resilience and Self-Compassion**: Mindfulness practices cultivate qualities of resilience, adaptability, and self-compassion, helping individuals with ADHD develop a more positive and accepting relationship with themselves and navigate life's challenges with greater ease.

Considerations for Practicing Mindfulness with ADHD:

1. **Individualized Approach**: Mindfulness interventions should be tailored to the unique needs, preferences, and characteristics of each individual with ADHD, considering factors such as attentional difficulties, hyperactivity, impulsivity, and emotional dysregulation.
2. **Structured and Supportive Environment**: Providing a structured and supportive environment for practicing mindfulness can enhance engagement and adherence, particularly for individuals with ADHD who may struggle with sustained attention or impulsivity.
3. **Integration with Other Treatments**: Mindfulness practices can complement other treatments for ADHD, such as medication management, behavioral therapy, and educational interventions, as part of a comprehensive and holistic approach to managing symptoms.
4. **Consistent Practice**: Consistent and regular practice of mindfulness is key to experiencing its benefits over time, emphasizing the importance of establishing a daily mindfulness routine and integrating mindfulness into daily activities and routines.

Coaching and counseling

Coaching for ADHD:

1. **Goal-Oriented Approach**: ADHD coaching emphasizes setting and achieving specific goals related to organization, time management, productivity, and self-regulation, tailored to the individual's unique needs and priorities.
2. **Skill Building**: Coaches provide practical strategies, tools, and techniques to help individuals with ADHD develop executive functioning skills, such as planning, prioritizing, problem-solving, and self-monitoring, to improve daily functioning and task performance.
3. **Accountability and Support**: Coaches offer accountability and support to help individuals with ADHD stay focused, motivated, and on track towards their goals, providing encouragement, feedback, and guidance throughout the coaching process.
4. **Problem-Solving and Decision-Making**: Coaches facilitate problem-solving and decision-making processes to help individuals with ADHD identify barriers, explore solutions, and make informed choices about managing their symptoms and achieving desired outcomes.
5. **Time Management and Organization**: Coaches assist individuals with ADHD in developing effective time management and organizational skills, creating structured routines, schedules, and systems to enhance productivity and reduce procrastination.

Counseling for ADHD:

1. **Emotional Support**: ADHD counseling provides a safe and supportive space for individuals to explore and process their emotions, experiences, and challenges related to

ADHD, helping them develop greater self-awareness and emotional regulation skills.

2. **Addressing Psychological Issues**: Counseling addresses psychological issues commonly associated with ADHD, such as low self-esteem, anxiety, depression, frustration, and stress, through evidence-based therapeutic interventions.

3. **Coping Strategies**: Counselors teach coping strategies and relaxation techniques to help individuals with ADHD manage stress, anxiety, and emotional dysregulation, promoting greater resilience and well-being.

4. **Improving Interpersonal Relationships**: Counseling helps individuals with ADHD improve communication skills, assertiveness, and conflict resolution abilities, enhancing their relationships with family members, peers, and colleagues.

5. **Identity and Self-Concept**: Counseling supports individuals with ADHD in exploring their identity, strengths, values, and aspirations, fostering a positive self-concept and sense of self-efficacy despite the challenges associated with the disorder.

Integration of Coaching and Counseling:

1. **Holistic Support**: Integrating coaching and counseling provides holistic support for individuals with ADHD, addressing both practical skill-building needs and emotional well-being to promote overall functioning and quality of life.

2. **Collaborative Approach**: Coaches and counselors can work collaboratively as part of a multidisciplinary team to provide coordinated care, sharing information, insights, and recommendations to support the individual's goals and treatment needs.

3. **Client-Centered Care**: The client's preferences, goals, and needs drive the integration of coaching and counseling, with interventions tailored to the individual's unique strengths, challenges, and circumstances.

4. **Continuum of Care**: Coaching and counseling can be offered as part of a continuum of care for individuals with ADHD, with services ranging from short-term skill-building interventions to long-term therapeutic support, depending on the individual's needs and treatment goals.

Chapter 09: Diet and Lifestyle

Impact of nutrition on ADHD symptoms

1. Role of Nutrients:

1. **Omega-3 Fatty Acids**: Omega-3 fatty acids, particularly eicosapentaenoic acid (EPA) and docosahexaenoic acid (DHA), are essential for brain health and cognitive function. Some studies suggest that supplementation with omega-3 fatty acids may improve ADHD symptoms, although findings are mixed.

2. **Micronutrients**: Certain micronutrients, including zinc, iron, magnesium, and vitamins B6, B9 (folate), and B12, play crucial roles in neurotransmitter synthesis, neural signaling, and energy metabolism. Deficiencies in these nutrients have been associated with ADHD symptoms, and supplementation may benefit some individuals.

3. **Protein**: Protein-rich foods provide amino acids, the building blocks of neurotransmitters such as dopamine and serotonin. Adequate protein intake may support neurotransmitter

balance and mood regulation, potentially influencing ADHD symptoms.

4. **Sugar and Additives**: Some studies suggest that high sugar intake and consumption of certain food additives, such as artificial colors, preservatives, and flavorings, may exacerbate hyperactivity and impulsivity in children with ADHD, although more research is needed to establish a clear link.

2. Dietary Patterns:

1. **Balanced Diet**: A well-balanced diet that includes a variety of nutrient-dense foods, such as fruits, vegetables, whole grains, lean proteins, and healthy fats, provides essential nutrients for brain health and supports overall functioning.
2. **Avoidance of Triggers**: Some individuals with ADHD may be sensitive to certain foods or additives that worsen symptoms. Identifying and avoiding potential dietary triggers, such as sugary snacks, processed foods, or artificial ingredients, may help mitigate symptom exacerbation.
3. **Meal Timing and Composition**: Consistent meal timing and composition, including regular intake of protein, complex carbohydrates, and healthy fats, can help stabilize blood sugar levels and sustain energy throughout the day, potentially improving attention and concentration.

3. Individual Variability:

1. **Genetic Factors**: Genetic variations may influence individual responses to dietary factors and their impact on ADHD symptoms. Personalized nutrition approaches that consider genetic predispositions

and metabolic differences may be more effective in optimizing dietary interventions for ADHD.

2. **Coexisting Conditions**: Individuals with ADHD may have coexisting conditions or dietary restrictions that affect their nutritional needs and dietary choices. Considering comorbidities such as allergies, sensitivities, or gastrointestinal issues is important when implementing dietary interventions.

4. Holistic Approach:

1. **Multimodal Treatment**: Nutrition should be considered as part of a multimodal treatment approach for ADHD, which may include medication management, behavioral interventions, educational support, and parent training programs. Integrating nutrition into a comprehensive treatment plan can enhance overall outcomes and well-being.

2. **Collaboration with Healthcare Providers**: Healthcare providers, including physicians, dietitians, and mental health professionals, can collaborate to assess dietary patterns, identify nutritional deficiencies or sensitivities, and develop personalized nutrition strategies tailored to the individual's needs and preferences.

Role of exercise and physical activity

1. Improved Cognitive Functioning:

1. **Enhanced Executive Functioning**: Exercise has been shown to improve executive functions such as working memory,

cognitive flexibility, inhibitory control, and planning abilities, which are often impaired in individuals with ADHD.

2. **Increased Attention and Focus**: Physical activity promotes the release of neurotransmitters such as dopamine, norepinephrine, and serotonin, which are involved in attention regulation and arousal, leading to improved focus and concentration.

2. Reduction of ADHD Symptoms:

1. **Decreased Hyperactivity and Impulsivity**: Regular exercise can help reduce hyperactive and impulsive behaviors by providing an outlet for excess energy, promoting self-regulation, and enhancing impulse control.
2. **Improved Self-Regulation**: Exercise fosters self-regulation skills by teaching individuals with ADHD to manage their impulses, emotions, and behavior in structured and goal-directed activities, both during and after physical activity.

3. Mood Regulation and Stress Reduction:

1. **Elevated Mood**: Physical activity stimulates the release of endorphins, neurotransmitters that promote feelings of happiness, relaxation, and well-being, which can help alleviate symptoms of depression, anxiety, and mood instability commonly associated with ADHD.
2. **Stress Reduction**: Exercise acts as a natural stress reliever, reducing levels of cortisol, the stress hormone, and promoting relaxation and emotional balance, thereby mitigating the negative impact of stress on ADHD symptoms.

4. Enhancement of Brain Structure and Function:

1. **Neuroplasticity**: Exercise has been shown to enhance neuroplasticity, the brain's ability to reorganize and adapt in response to experience, leading to structural and functional changes that support cognitive development, learning, and memory.
2. **Brain-Derived Neurotrophic Factor (BDNF)**: Physical activity increases the production of BDNF, a protein that supports neuronal growth, survival, and synaptic plasticity, contributing to improved brain health and cognitive functioning in individuals with ADHD.

5. Promotion of Healthy Lifestyle Habits:

1. **Sleep Quality**: Regular exercise can improve sleep quality and duration, reducing insomnia and sleep disturbances commonly experienced by individuals with ADHD, which in turn may enhance daytime functioning and attentional performance.
2. **Healthy Weight Management**: Engaging in physical activity helps maintain a healthy weight and reduces the risk of obesity, a common concern among individuals with ADHD due to potential medication side effects and sedentary behavior.

6. Social Engagement and Peer Interaction:

1. **Social Skills Development**: Participating in team sports, group activities, or exercise classes provides opportunities for social interaction, teamwork, cooperation, and communication skills development, which can benefit individuals with ADHD in building positive relationships and social connections.
2. **Peer Support**: Exercise environments offer opportunities for peer support, acceptance, and inclusion, providing a sense of belonging and camaraderie that can boost self-esteem and confidence in individuals with ADHD.

Considerations for Implementation:

1. **Individual Preferences**: Encourage individuals with ADHD to choose physical activities that align with their interests, preferences, and abilities, whether it's team sports, outdoor activities, dance, martial arts, or individual pursuits like biking or hiking.
2. **Consistency and Routine**: Establishing a consistent exercise routine and incorporating physical activity into daily life can maximize the benefits of exercise for ADHD symptoms, promoting habit formation and sustainable behavior change.
3. **Gradual Progression**: Start with manageable and enjoyable activities, gradually increasing intensity, duration, and complexity over time to prevent overwhelm and promote adherence to exercise goals.
4. **Family and Social Support**: Engage family members, caregivers, peers, and support networks in promoting physical activity and providing encouragement, motivation, and reinforcement for participation in exercise-related activities.

5. **Integration with Treatment**: Integrate exercise and physical activity as part of a comprehensive treatment plan for ADHD, complementing other interventions such as medication management, behavioral therapy, education, and dietary modifications.

By incorporating regular exercise and physical activity into their daily routines, individuals with ADHD can harness the therapeutic benefits of movement to optimize cognitive functioning, mood regulation, stress management, and overall well-being, enhancing their ability to thrive and succeed in various life domains.

Sleep and its effects on ADHD

1. Prevalence of Sleep Problems:

1. **Insomnia**: Individuals with ADHD are more likely to experience difficulty falling asleep, staying asleep, or waking up too early, leading to insomnia symptoms and poor sleep quality.
2. **Delayed Sleep Phase Syndrome**: Some individuals with ADHD may have a delayed sleep-wake phase, characterized by a tendency to go to bed and wake up later than desired, which can disrupt sleep schedules and affect daytime functioning.
3. **Restless Legs Syndrome (RLS) and Periodic Limb Movement Disorder (PLMD)**: ADHD is associated with a higher prevalence of RLS and PLMD, which involve uncomfortable sensations or involuntary movements in the legs during sleep, leading to sleep fragmentation and daytime fatigue.
4. **Obstructive Sleep Apnea (OSA)**: Although less common, individuals with ADHD may also be at increased risk for OSA, a sleep-related breathing disorder characterized by repetitive episodes of partial or complete upper airway obstruction

during sleep, which can impair sleep quality and contribute to daytime sleepiness and cognitive deficits.

2. Impact on ADHD Symptoms:

1. **Attention and Concentration**: Sleep deprivation and poor sleep quality can exacerbate symptoms of inattention, distractibility, and cognitive deficits associated with ADHD, impairing attentional performance and academic or occupational functioning.
2. **Hyperactivity and Impulsivity**: Sleep disturbances may worsen hyperactive and impulsive behaviors, leading to increased restlessness, fidgeting, and impulsivity during waking hours, which can interfere with daily activities and social interactions.
3. **Emotional Regulation**: Inadequate sleep can impair emotional regulation and mood stability, exacerbating irritability, mood swings, emotional lability, and stress reactivity commonly observed in individuals with ADHD.
4. **Executive Functioning**: Sleep deprivation can compromise executive functioning skills such as planning, organization, problem-solving, and decision-making, further impairing cognitive flexibility and adaptive behavior in individuals with ADHD.

3. Bidirectional Relationship:

1. **Sleep Problems as a Risk Factor**: Sleep disturbances in childhood may precede the onset of ADHD symptoms or exacerbate existing ADHD symptoms, suggesting a bidirectional relationship between sleep and ADHD.
2. **Impact of ADHD Treatment on Sleep**: Medications commonly used to treat ADHD, such as stimulants or

non-stimulants, may affect sleep patterns and contribute to sleep disturbances, although the extent and nature of these effects vary among individuals.

4. Treatment and Management:

1. **Sleep Hygiene Practices**: Implementing good sleep hygiene practices, such as maintaining a consistent sleep schedule, creating a relaxing bedtime routine, limiting screen time before bed, and optimizing sleep environment (e.g., comfortable bedding, dark and quiet room), can promote better sleep quality and quantity.
2. **Behavioral Interventions**: Cognitive-behavioral therapy for insomnia (CBT-I) or behavioral interventions targeting sleep problems may be beneficial for individuals with ADHD who experience chronic sleep disturbances, addressing underlying factors contributing to sleep difficulties.
3. **Medication Management**: Healthcare providers may consider adjusting ADHD medications or prescribing adjunctive treatments to manage sleep disturbances while optimizing symptom control, taking into account individual preferences, tolerability, and treatment response.
4. **Comprehensive Assessment**: Comprehensive assessment of sleep patterns, habits, and symptoms is essential for identifying and addressing sleep problems in individuals with ADHD, ensuring that sleep-related issues are adequately addressed as part of their overall treatment plan.

Chapter 10: ADHD and Gender Differences

How ADHD presents differently in males and females

1. Symptom Expression:

1. **Inattention**:
- **Males**: Inattentive symptoms in males with ADHD may manifest as difficulty sustaining attention on tasks, forgetfulness, disorganization, and poor task completion.
- **Females**: Females with ADHD may exhibit less overt inattentive behaviors and may internalize their symptoms, leading to difficulties with organization, time management, and self-regulation.
2. **Hyperactivity and Impulsivity**:
- **Males**: Hyperactive-impulsive symptoms in males with ADHD tend to be more externalized and evident, characterized by excessive fidgeting, restlessness, impulsivity, and risk-taking behaviors.
- **Females**: Females with ADHD may display less overt hyperactive and impulsive behaviors and may present with symptoms such as impulsivity in social contexts, internal restlessness, or excessive talking.

2. Diagnostic Patterns:

1. **Underdiagnosis in Females**: ADHD is often underdiagnosed in females, particularly those who present with predominantly inattentive symptoms or exhibit compensatory coping mechanisms that mask their difficulties, such as perfectionism or hyperfocus.
2. **Delayed Diagnosis**: Females with ADHD may receive a diagnosis later in life compared to males, as their symptoms may be attributed to other conditions (e.g., anxiety, depression) or overlooked due to gender biases and societal expectations.

3. Comorbidities:

1. **Internalizing Disorders**: Females with ADHD are more likely to have comorbid internalizing disorders such as anxiety, depression, and low self-esteem, which may overshadow or complicate the presentation of ADHD symptoms.
2. **Externalizing Behaviors in Males**: Males with ADHD are more likely to exhibit comorbid externalizing behaviors such as oppositional defiant disorder (ODD), conduct disorder (CD), or substance use disorders, which may contribute to disruptive or antisocial behaviors.

4. Social and Academic Functioning:

1. **Social Impairments**: Females with ADHD may experience social difficulties characterized by rejection, peer conflict, and feelings of loneliness, often due to subtle social cues or communication challenges.
2. **Academic Underachievement**: Both males and females with ADHD may struggle academically, but females are more likely to exhibit internalizing behaviors (e.g., withdrawal, disengagement) that contribute to academic underachievement, while males may display externalizing behaviors (e.g., disruptive behavior, defiance).

5. Coping Mechanisms and Masking:

1. **Compensatory Strategies**: Females with ADHD may develop compensatory strategies to cope with their symptoms, such as perfectionism, overachievement, or seeking support from peers, which may temporarily mitigate their difficulties but contribute to stress and burnout over time.
2. **Masking Behaviors**: Both males and females with ADHD may engage in masking behaviors to conceal their symptoms in certain contexts, such as social situations or academic settings, leading to internalized stress and feelings of inadequacy.

Gender-specific challenges and strengths

1. Gender-Specific Challenges:

Males:

1. **Externalizing Behaviors**: Males with ADHD are more likely to exhibit externalizing behaviors such as hyperactivity, impulsivity, aggression, and disruptive behavior, which may lead to disciplinary issues, academic underachievement, and conflicts with authority figures.
2. **Social Difficulties**: Males with ADHD may experience challenges in social interactions and peer relationships, characterized by difficulties with social skills, social perception, and perspective-taking, leading to social rejection, isolation, and feelings of loneliness.

3. **Risk-Taking Behaviors**: Males with ADHD are more prone to engaging in risk-taking behaviors such as substance abuse, reckless driving, and delinquent activities, which may result from impulsivity, sensation-seeking tendencies, and poor decision-making skills.

Females:

1. **Underdiagnosis and Misdiagnosis**: ADHD is often underdiagnosed or misdiagnosed in females, particularly those who present with predominantly inattentive symptoms or exhibit internalizing behaviors such as anxiety, depression, or emotional dysregulation, leading to delayed or missed treatment opportunities.
2. **Compensatory Coping Strategies**: Females with ADHD may develop compensatory coping strategies such as perfectionism, overachievement, or people-pleasing behaviors to mask their symptoms and meet societal expectations, which may contribute to stress, burnout, and feelings of inadequacy.
3. **Social Isolation**: Females with ADHD may experience social difficulties characterized by rejection, peer conflict, and difficulties in forming and maintaining friendships, often due to subtle social cues, communication challenges, or social anxiety.

2. Gender-Specific Strengths:

Males:

1. **Physical Energy and Activity**: Males with ADHD often possess high levels of physical energy and activity, which can be channeled into sports,

outdoor activities, or hands-on tasks, providing opportunities for engagement, self-expression, and stress relief.

2. **Creativity and Problem-Solving**: Males with ADHD may demonstrate creativity, innovation, and out-of-the-box thinking, leveraging their ability to think divergently and generate novel ideas in various domains such as art, engineering, or entrepreneurship.

Females:

1. **Emotional Intelligence**: Females with ADHD may exhibit strengths in emotional intelligence, empathy, and interpersonal sensitivity, allowing them to connect with others on a deeper level, provide emotional support, and navigate complex social dynamics with insight and understanding.

2. **Adaptability and Resilience**: Females with ADHD often demonstrate adaptability, resilience, and resourcefulness in managing their symptoms and overcoming challenges, drawing upon their ability to persevere, problem-solve, and find creative solutions to obstacles.

Tailoring interventions to gender differences

1. Gender-Sensitive Assessment:

1. **Comprehensive Evaluation**: Conduct a thorough assessment that considers gender-specific differences in ADHD presentation, symptom expression, and comorbidities, using

validated screening tools, clinical interviews, and collateral information from multiple sources.

2. **Cultural Sensitivity**: Be sensitive to cultural and social factors that may influence the perception and expression of ADHD symptoms in males and females, recognizing the impact of gender norms, stereotypes, and societal expectations on symptom manifestation.

2. Differential Diagnosis:

1. **Recognition of Atypical Presentations**: Be vigilant for atypical presentations of ADHD in females, such as predominantly inattentive symptoms, internalizing behaviors, or compensatory coping strategies, which may differ from the classic hyperactive-impulsive presentation typically seen in males.

2. **Screening for Comorbidities**: Screen for common comorbidities associated with ADHD, such as anxiety, depression, and eating disorders, which may be more prevalent in females and may require targeted assessment and intervention.

3. Individualized Treatment Planning:

1. **Multimodal Approach**: Develop a comprehensive treatment plan that incorporates a combination of pharmacological, behavioral, educational, and psychosocial interventions tailored to the individual's unique profile, needs, preferences, and gender-specific challenges.

2. **Medication Management**: Consider individualized medication management strategies based on gender-specific symptom profiles, treatment response, tolerability, and potential side effects,

with ongoing monitoring and adjustments as needed.

4. Behavioral Interventions:

1. **Skill-Building Programs**: Implement behavioral interventions targeting executive functioning skills, social skills, emotion regulation, and adaptive coping strategies, adapting the content and delivery to resonate with the experiences and preferences of males and females with ADHD.
2. **Parent Training and Education**: Provide gender-sensitive parent training programs that address parenting challenges specific to ADHD in males and females, emphasizing effective communication, discipline strategies, and family support systems.

5. Educational Support:

1. **Individualized Education Plans (IEPs)**: Develop IEPs that accommodate gender-specific learning styles, strengths, and challenges, providing academic accommodations, modifications, and supports tailored to the individual's needs and educational goals.
2. **Teacher Training and Collaboration**: Offer professional development and support for educators in recognizing and addressing gender differences in ADHD, fostering inclusive classroom environments, and implementing evidence-based teaching

strategies that accommodate diverse learning needs.

6. Psychosocial Support:

1. **Group Therapy and Support Groups**: Facilitate gender-specific group therapy or support groups for individuals with ADHD, providing opportunities for peer support, social connection, and validation of shared experiences, while addressing gender-related concerns and issues.
2. **Counseling and Psychotherapy**: Offer individual or family counseling that integrates gender-sensitive approaches, addressing identity development, self-esteem, body image, relationship dynamics, and other psychosocial factors that may impact ADHD management and well-being.

Chapter 11: Parenting a Child with ADHD

Parenting strategies and support

1. Psychoeducation and Understanding ADHD:

1. **Learn About ADHD**: Educate yourself about ADHD, including its symptoms, causes, treatment options, and potential impact on your child's functioning and behavior. Understanding the nature of ADHD can help you better support your child and advocate for their needs.
2. **Provide Age-Appropriate Information**: Explain ADHD to your child in age-appropriate language, helping them understand their diagnosis, strengths, challenges, and the strategies they can use to manage their symptoms effectively.

2. Positive Parenting Techniques:

1. **Consistent Structure and Routine**: Establish clear and consistent rules, routines, and expectations at home, providing structure and predictability for your child. Use visual schedules, checklists, and timers to help your child stay organized and manage transitions.
2. **Positive Reinforcement**: Use praise, encouragement, and rewards to reinforce positive behaviors and accomplishments, focusing on your child's strengths and efforts rather than just their challenges.
3. **Effective Discipline Strategies**: Use proactive and positive discipline strategies that focus on teaching and guiding your child's behavior rather than punitive measures. Set clear limits, offer choices, and use logical consequences that are related to your child's actions.

3. Communication and Relationship Building:

1. **Open Communication**: Maintain open and honest communication with your child, providing a supportive and nonjudgmental environment where they feel comfortable expressing their thoughts, feelings, and concerns.
2. **Active Listening**: Practice active listening skills, empathizing with your child's experiences and validating their emotions. Encourage your child to share their perspectives and collaborate on problem-solving together.

4. Collaboration with School and Healthcare Providers:

1. **Collaborate with Teachers**: Work closely with your child's teachers and school staff to develop a collaborative partnership in supporting your child's academic, social, and behavioral needs. Share information about your child's ADHD, effective strategies, and accommodations that may be helpful in the classroom.
2. **Consult with Healthcare Providers**: Regularly consult with healthcare providers, including pediatricians, psychiatrists, psychologists, and therapists, to monitor your child's progress, adjust treatment plans as needed, and access additional support services.

5. Self-Care and Support for Parents:

1. **Self-Care Practices**: Prioritize self-care and well-being as a parent, taking time to recharge, rest, and engage in activities that bring you joy and relaxation. Maintain a healthy balance between caregiving responsibilities and personal needs.
2. **Parent Support Groups**: Seek support from other parents of children with ADHD through support groups, online forums, or parent education programs. Connecting with peers who understand your experiences can provide validation, empathy, and practical advice.

6. Building Resilience and Coping Skills:

1. **Promote Resilience**: Foster resilience and self-confidence in your child by highlighting their strengths, teaching problem-solving skills, and emphasizing the importance of perseverance and resilience in overcoming challenges.
2. **Teach Coping Strategies**: Teach your child coping strategies and relaxation techniques to manage stress, frustration, and impulsivity. Encourage mindfulness, deep breathing exercises, and physical activities that promote self-regulation.

Building a positive home environment

1. Establish Clear Structure and Routine:

1. **Consistent Schedule**: Establish a consistent daily routine with set times for waking up, meals, homework, chores, playtime, and bedtime. Use visual schedules, charts, or calendars to help your child understand and follow the routine.
2. **Predictable Environment**: Create a predictable environment with clear expectations, rules, and consequences. Consistency and predictability can help reduce stress and anxiety for children with ADHD, providing a sense of security and stability.

2. Foster a Supportive Atmosphere:

1. **Encourage Open Communication**: Create an environment where your child feels comfortable expressing their thoughts, feelings, and concerns without fear of judgment or criticism. Listen actively, validate their emotions, and offer reassurance and encouragement.

2. **Focus on Strengths**: Recognize and celebrate your child's strengths, talents, and achievements. Encourage their interests, passions, and areas of success, fostering a sense of self-confidence and self-worth.

3. Promote Positive Reinforcement:

1. **Use Positive Reinforcement**: Reinforce positive behaviors and accomplishments with praise, encouragement, and rewards. Focus on your child's efforts and progress, rather than just the outcomes, to build self-esteem and motivation.
2. **Create a Reward System**: Establish a reward system that incentivizes desired behaviors and goals. Allow your child to earn privileges, privileges, or special privileges through consistent demonstration of positive behaviors and adherence to rules.

4. Provide Structure and Support:

1. **Set Clear Expectations**: Clearly communicate your expectations for behavior, chores, and responsibilities. Break tasks into manageable steps, provide clear instructions, and offer guidance and support as needed.
2. **Teach Problem-Solving Skills**: Help your child develop problem-solving skills and coping strategies to manage challenges and setbacks. Encourage brainstorming, decision-making, and seeking help when needed, fostering independence and resilience.

5. Create a Calm and Organized Environment:

1. **Minimize Distractions**: Create a calm and organized environment with minimal distractions to help your child stay focused and attentive. Limit screen time, reduce clutter, and designate quiet spaces for homework and relaxation.
2. **Establish Clear Routines**: Implement daily routines for tasks such as getting ready for school, completing homework, and winding down before bedtime. Provide visual cues, checklists, or timers to help your child stay on track and manage time effectively.

6. Practice Self-Care and Patience:

1. **Take Care of Yourself**: Prioritize self-care and well-being as a parent, managing your stress, and seeking support when needed. Take breaks, engage in hobbies, and maintain a healthy balance between caregiving responsibilities and personal needs.
2. **Practice Patience and Empathy**: Be patient and understanding with your child, recognizing that managing ADHD symptoms can be challenging for them. Offer empathy, support, and encouragement, and avoid criticism or negative judgments.

1. Prioritize Self-Care:

1. **Take Breaks**: Allow yourself regular breaks throughout the day to rest, recharge, and engage in activities that you enjoy. Even short periods of relaxation can help reduce stress and prevent burnout.
2. **Maintain Healthy Habits**: Prioritize your physical and mental health by eating a balanced diet, getting regular exercise, and practicing relaxation techniques such as deep breathing, meditation, or yoga.
3. **Get Adequate Sleep**: Ensure you're getting enough sleep each night to replenish your energy and support your overall well-being. Establish a consistent sleep routine and create a conducive sleep environment to improve sleep quality.

2. Seek Social Support:

1. **Connect with Others**: Reach out to friends, family members, or support groups for emotional support, understanding, and encouragement. Sharing your experiences with others who can relate can help alleviate feelings of isolation and provide a sense of camaraderie.
2. **Join Parenting Groups**: Consider joining parenting groups or online forums specifically for parents of children with ADHD. These communities can offer valuable insights, practical tips, and a sense of solidarity with others facing similar challenges.

3. Set Realistic Expectations:

1. **Accept Imperfection**: Recognize that it's okay to not have all the answers or to make mistakes as a parent. Embrace imperfection and adopt a mindset of self-compassion, allowing yourself grace and understanding during challenging times.
2. **Focus on Progress, Not Perfection**: Shift your focus from achieving perfection to making progress. Celebrate small victories, improvements, and efforts, acknowledging the steps you're taking to support your child and yourself.

4. Practice Stress Management Techniques:

1. **Mindfulness and Relaxation**: Incorporate mindfulness practices and relaxation techniques into your daily routine to help manage stress and promote emotional well-being. Practice mindfulness meditation, deep breathing exercises, or progressive muscle relaxation to cultivate a sense of calm and inner peace.
2. **Time Management**: Use effective time management strategies to prioritize tasks, set realistic goals, and allocate time for self-care and relaxation. Break tasks into smaller, manageable steps, and delegate responsibilities when possible to lighten your workload.

5. Communicate and Collaborate:

1. **Open Communication**: Maintain open and honest communication with your child,

partner, and healthcare providers about your needs, concerns, and challenges. Expressing your feelings and seeking support can help alleviate stress and foster a sense of connection and understanding.
2. **Collaborate with Your Child's Team**: Work collaboratively with your child's teachers, therapists, and healthcare providers to develop a comprehensive support plan that addresses your child's needs at home, school, and in the community. Keep lines of communication open and advocate for your child's best interests.

6. Take Breaks and Practice Self-Compassion:

1. **Respite Care**: Consider arranging respite care or childcare services to give yourself periodic breaks from caregiving responsibilities. Taking time for yourself allows you to recharge and maintain your own well-being.
2. **Practice Self-Compassion**: Be kind to yourself and acknowledge the challenges you're facing as a parent of a child with ADHD. Practice self-compassion by treating yourself with the same care, understanding, and support that you would offer to a friend in a similar situation.

Chapter 12: ADHD and Technology Use

Impact of video games and social media

1. Impact of Video Games:

Potential Benefits:

1. **Enhanced Cognitive Skills**: Certain video games can help improve cognitive skills such as problem-solving, spatial awareness, and strategic thinking. Games that require planning, multitasking, and quick decision-making can be particularly beneficial.
2. **Social Interaction**: Multiplayer and online games can provide opportunities for social interaction, cooperation, and teamwork. This can help children with ADHD develop social skills and build friendships in a structured environment.
3. **Stress Relief**: Video games can offer a form of escapism and stress relief, providing children with a fun and engaging way to relax and unwind.

Potential Challenges:

1. **Hyperfocus**: Children with ADHD may become hyperfocused on video games, leading to excessive screen time and difficulty disengaging from the activity. This can result in neglect of other responsibilities, such as homework, chores, and social interactions.
2. **Impulsivity and Aggression**: Some video games, particularly those with violent content, may exacerbate impulsivity and aggressive behaviors in children with ADHD. Exposure to such content can lead to increased irritability and difficulties in emotional regulation.

3. **Sleep Disruption**: Excessive video game use, especially before bedtime, can disrupt sleep patterns and negatively affect sleep quality. Poor sleep can worsen ADHD symptoms, such as inattention, hyperactivity, and irritability.

2. Impact of Social Media:

Potential Benefits:

1. **Social Connection**: Social media platforms can help children with ADHD stay connected with friends and family, providing a sense of belonging and social support. They can also be a valuable tool for finding communities of interest and support groups.
2. **Educational Resources**: Social media can be a source of educational content and resources, helping children with ADHD access information and learn new skills in an engaging format.
3. **Self-Expression**: Social media offers a platform for self-expression and creativity, allowing children to share their thoughts, interests, and achievements with a wider audience.

Potential Challenges:

1. **Distraction and Inattention**: The constant notifications and updates on social media can be highly distracting for children with ADHD, leading to difficulties in sustaining attention and focusing on tasks.
2. **Social Comparison and Self-Esteem**: Social media can contribute to negative self-

comparison and low self-esteem, as children with ADHD may compare themselves to others and feel inadequate or left out.

3. **Cyberbullying and Online Risks**: Children with ADHD may be more vulnerable to cyberbullying, online harassment, and exposure to inappropriate content. Their impulsivity may also lead to risky online behaviors, such as sharing personal information.

3. Strategies for Managing Video Game and Social Media Use:

1. **Set Limits and Boundaries**: Establish clear rules and time limits for video game and social media use. Use tools such as timers, parental controls, and screen time management apps to help enforce these limits.

2. **Create a Balanced Schedule**: Encourage a balanced daily schedule that includes time for physical activities, homework, chores, family interactions, and screen-free relaxation. Ensure that digital activities do not interfere with essential routines, such as sleep and meals.

3. **Monitor Content**: Monitor the content of video games and social media platforms to ensure it is age-appropriate and aligns with your family values. Encourage the use of educational and positive content that supports learning and personal growth.

4. **Promote Offline Activities**: Encourage your child to engage in offline activities that

promote social interaction, physical exercise, and creative expression. This can include sports, hobbies, reading, and family outings.

5. **Model Healthy Behavior**: Model healthy screen habits by setting a good example with your own video game and social media use. Show your child the importance of balancing screen time with other activities.

6. **Open Communication**: Maintain open and honest communication with your child about the potential benefits and risks of video games and social media. Discuss appropriate online behavior, privacy, and how to handle negative experiences, such as cyberbullying.

7. **Teach Self-Regulation**: Help your child develop self-regulation skills by teaching them to recognize signs of excessive use and take breaks when needed. Encourage mindfulness and self-awareness to help them manage their screen time effectively.

Balancing technology use

1. Set Clear Rules and Boundaries

1. **Establish Time Limits**: Define specific time limits for different types of technology use, such as gaming, social media, and educational activities. Use timers and parental control apps to help enforce these limits.

2. **Create a Technology Schedule**: Develop a daily or weekly schedule that allocates specific times for technology use. This schedule should balance screen time with other activities such as homework, chores, physical exercise, and family time.

3. **Designate Tech-Free Zones**: Identify areas in the home, such as the dining room and bedrooms, where technology use is restricted. This helps create spaces for family interaction and rest without digital distractions.

2. Encourage Healthy Technology Use

1. **Educational Content**: Prioritize educational apps, games, and programs that support learning and development. Encourage your child to use technology for school projects, reading, and skill-building activities.
2. **Positive Social Interaction**: Guide your child towards using social media and online platforms for positive interactions, such as connecting with friends, participating in interest-based groups, and engaging in collaborative projects.
3. **Mindful Consumption**: Teach your child to be mindful of their technology use by recognizing when they feel overwhelmed or overstimulated. Encourage them to take breaks and engage in offline activities when needed.

3. Monitor and Supervise

1. **Regular Check-Ins**: Regularly check in with your child about their technology use. Discuss what apps and games they are using, who they are interacting with online, and any issues or concerns they may have.
2. **Parental Controls**: Utilize parental control features available on devices and apps to monitor and restrict content. These tools can help block inappropriate content and limit screen time.
3. **Co-Use Technology**: Spend time using technology together with your child. This can include playing video games, exploring educational apps, or

watching movies. Co-use provides an opportunity to model healthy habits and discuss content.

4. Promote Alternative Activities

1. **Physical Exercise**: Encourage regular physical activity by involving your child in sports, outdoor play, and other physical hobbies. Exercise helps manage ADHD symptoms and provides a healthy balance to screen time.
2. **Creative Outlets**: Foster creative activities such as drawing, painting, writing, music, or building projects. These activities can be a productive and enjoyable alternative to screen time.
3. **Family Time**: Plan regular family activities that do not involve screens, such as board games, cooking together, hiking, or visiting local attractions. These activities help strengthen family bonds and provide a break from technology.

5. Model Healthy Behavior

1. **Set an Example**: Demonstrate balanced technology use by adhering to the same rules and limits you set for your child. Show that you also prioritize offline activities and maintain a healthy relationship with technology.
2. **Digital Detox**: Occasionally take a "digital detox" as a family by designating certain times or days as screen-free. Use this time to reconnect and engage in meaningful offline activities together.

3. **Discuss Tech Use**: Openly discuss the pros and cons of technology use with your child. Share your own experiences and encourage them to reflect on how technology affects their mood, behavior, and relationships.

6. Foster Self-Regulation and Accountability

1. **Teach Self-Regulation**: Help your child develop self-regulation skills by teaching them to set their own limits and recognize when they need a break from screens. Encourage them to use techniques such as setting timers or creating tech-free periods.
2. **Goal Setting**: Work with your child to set goals related to their technology use, such as limiting screen time during weekdays or completing homework before gaming. Celebrate their achievements and provide positive reinforcement.
3. **Responsibility and Independence**: Gradually give your child more responsibility and independence in managing their technology use. Encourage them to make informed decisions and be accountable for their choices.

Utilizing technology for ADHD management

1. Organizational Tools

1. **Digital Planners and Calendars**: Apps like Google Calendar, Microsoft Outlook, and Apple Calendar can help individuals with ADHD keep track of appointments, deadlines, and daily tasks. Setting reminders and alarms can ensure important events and tasks are not forgotten.
2. **Task Management Apps**: Applications like Todoist, Trello, and Asana provide platforms to create to-do lists, set priorities, and track progress. These apps often include features like

deadlines, recurring tasks, and project management capabilities that can help users stay organized and manage their time effectively.

3. **Note-Taking Apps**: Tools like Evernote, OneNote, and Notion allow users to take notes, store information, and organize thoughts in a structured manner. These apps can be particularly useful for managing schoolwork, projects, and personal tasks.

2. Focus and Attention Aids

1. **Pomodoro Timers**: Apps like Focus Booster and Pomodone employ the Pomodoro Technique, which involves working in short, focused intervals (typically 25 minutes) followed by a short break. This method can help individuals with ADHD maintain concentration and productivity.
2. **White Noise and Ambient Sound Apps**: Background noise apps like Noisli, White Noise, and Calm can create a conducive environment for focus by masking distracting sounds. These apps offer various soundscapes such as rain, forest, and ocean waves.
3. **Distraction-Blocking Apps**: Tools like Freedom, Cold Turkey, and StayFocusd can block distracting websites and apps during work or study periods. These apps help minimize interruptions and enhance focus on the task at hand.

3. Educational and Cognitive Training Apps

1. **Memory and Cognitive Skills Training**: Apps like Lumosity and CogniFit offer brain training exercises designed to improve cognitive functions such as memory, attention, and problem-solving skills.

Regular use of these apps can help enhance cognitive abilities in individuals with ADHD.

2. **Educational Apps**: Platforms like Khan Academy, Quizlet, and Duolingo provide interactive and engaging learning experiences. These apps can help children and adults with ADHD learn new concepts and reinforce knowledge in a structured and enjoyable manner.

3. **Gamified Learning**: Educational games such as Prodigy (math) and BrainPOP (various subjects) use game-based learning to keep students engaged and motivated. Gamification can make learning more appealing and effective for those with ADHD.

4. Behavioral and Emotional Regulation

1. **Mindfulness and Meditation Apps**: Apps like Headspace, Calm, and Insight Timer offer guided meditation, mindfulness exercises, and breathing techniques that can help manage stress, anxiety, and impulsivity. Regular practice can improve emotional regulation and overall mental well-being.

2. **Mood Tracking Apps**: Tools like Daylio and Moodpath allow users to track their moods and identify patterns over time. These apps can provide insights into emotional triggers and help develop strategies for managing emotions effectively.

3. **Behavior Tracking**: Apps like Behavior Tracker Pro and ClassDojo can help monitor and reinforce positive behaviors in children with ADHD. These tools can be used by parents and teachers to track behavior progress and implement reward systems.

5. Communication and Collaboration

1. **Communication Apps**: Tools like Slack, Microsoft Teams, and WhatsApp facilitate communication and collaboration among family members, teachers, and therapists. These apps can be used to share updates, set reminders, and coordinate activities.
2. **Virtual Therapy**: Teletherapy platforms like BetterHelp and Talkspace offer convenient access to therapy and counseling services. These platforms provide support for managing ADHD symptoms, emotional challenges, and developing coping strategies.
3. **Educational Support**: Apps like Remind and ClassTag facilitate communication between parents, students, and teachers, ensuring that everyone is informed about assignments, events, and student progress.

6. Health and Wellness

1. **Fitness and Exercise Apps**: Apps like MyFitnessPal, Fitbit, and Nike Training Club offer workout plans, activity tracking, and nutrition advice. Regular physical activity can help manage ADHD symptoms by improving focus, reducing impulsivity, and promoting overall well-being.
2. **Sleep Tracking**: Tools like Sleep Cycle and Fitbit provide insights into sleep patterns and quality. Good sleep hygiene is crucial for managing ADHD symptoms, and these apps can help users establish and maintain healthy sleep routines.
3. **Diet and Nutrition**: Apps like Yummly and MyPlate can help plan and track balanced diets. Proper nutrition plays a

significant role in managing ADHD, and these apps can guide individuals towards healthier eating habits.

Chapter 13: Living Well with ADHD

Embracing strengths and managing challenges

Embracing Strengths

1. **Creativity and Innovation**: Many individuals with ADHD are highly creative and think outside the box. They often bring unique perspectives and innovative ideas to problem-solving and creative projects.
   - **Encouragement**: Encourage participation in activities that foster creativity, such as art, music, writing, or design. Provide opportunities for creative expression and celebrate innovative thinking.
   - **Projects and Hobbies**: Support engagement in personal projects and hobbies that allow for creative exploration and development.
2. **High Energy and Enthusiasm**: The high energy levels associated with ADHD can be channeled into positive, productive activities.
   - **Active Tasks**: Involve individuals in tasks that require movement and physical activity, such as sports, dance, or hands-on projects.
   - **Passionate Interests**: Encourage pursuits in areas of strong interest, where enthusiasm can be harnessed to achieve excellence and mastery.
3. **Resilience and Adaptability**: Many individuals with ADHD develop resilience and adaptability through navigating their challenges.
   - **Building Resilience**: Highlight past successes and strategies that have worked well, reinforcing a growth mindset.
   - **Adaptable Tasks**: Provide opportunities to practice adaptability through tasks that require problem-solving and quick thinking.

4. **Hyperfocus**: While ADHD is often associated with inattention, individuals can also experience periods of hyperfocus on activities they find particularly engaging.
   - **Focused Activities**: Identify activities and tasks that naturally capture attention and allow for deep engagement.
   - **Balancing Hyperfocus**: Teach strategies to manage hyperfocus, ensuring it is directed towards productive activities and balanced with other responsibilities.

Managing Challenges

1. **Inattention and Distractibility**: Difficulty maintaining attention and being easily distracted are common challenges.
   - **Structured Environment**: Create a structured and organized environment with minimal distractions. Use tools like checklists, timers, and planners to aid focus.
   - **Break Tasks**: Break tasks into smaller, manageable steps with clear, short-term goals. Provide frequent breaks to prevent burnout.
2. **Impulsivity**: Impulsive behaviors can lead to challenges in social interactions and decision-making.
   - **Impulse Control Techniques**: Teach techniques such as pausing before responding, using self-talk, and practicing mindfulness to enhance impulse control.
   - **Positive Outlets**: Provide positive outlets for energy and impulsivity, such as sports, physical activities, and creative expression.
3. **Hyperactivity**: High levels of physical activity can be disruptive in certain settings.
   - **Physical Activity**: Incorporate regular physical activity into the daily routine to help manage hyperactivity. Activities like running, swimming, and team sports can be beneficial.
   - **Fidget Tools**: Use fidget tools or allow movement breaks during sedentary activities to help manage restlessness.
4. **Organizational Difficulties**: Keeping track of tasks, deadlines, and belongings can be challenging.

- o **Organizational Systems**: Implement organizational systems such as labeled storage, color-coded folders, and digital reminders. Encourage routines for daily tasks.
- o **Support and Guidance**: Provide support and guidance in developing organizational skills, such as creating to-do lists and using planners effectively.

Strategies for Parents, Teachers, and Caregivers

1. **Positive Reinforcement**: Use positive reinforcement to encourage desired behaviors and achievements. Praise efforts, provide rewards, and celebrate successes.
2. **Clear Communication**: Communicate expectations clearly and consistently. Use visual aids, written instructions, and step-by-step guidance to enhance understanding.
3. **Collaborative Approach**: Work collaboratively with the individual, their teachers, and healthcare providers to develop a comprehensive support plan. Regularly review and adjust strategies as needed.
4. **Empathy and Patience**: Show empathy and patience, recognizing that managing ADHD can be challenging. Offer support, understanding, and encouragement.

Strategies for Individuals with ADHD

1. **Self-Awareness**: Develop self-awareness about ADHD and its impact. Understand personal strengths and challenges, and identify strategies that work best.
2. **Time Management**: Use time management tools and techniques, such as setting alarms, using calendars, and breaking tasks into smaller steps. Prioritize tasks and set realistic goals.
3. **Healthy Lifestyle**: Maintain a healthy lifestyle with regular exercise, balanced nutrition, and adequate

sleep. These factors can significantly impact ADHD symptoms.

4. **Mindfulness and Relaxation**: Practice mindfulness and relaxation techniques to manage stress and enhance focus. Activities like meditation, deep breathing, and yoga can be beneficial.
5. **Support Networks**: Build a support network of family, friends, teachers, and professionals who understand and support ADHD. Seek out support groups and resources for additional guidance.

Building a support network

1. Family Support

1. **Open Communication**: Maintain open and honest communication within the family. Regularly discuss challenges, progress, and strategies that are working or need adjustment.
   - **Family Meetings**: Hold regular family meetings to discuss schedules, responsibilities, and any issues related to ADHD management.
   - **Active Listening**: Encourage active listening, ensuring everyone feels heard and understood.
2. **Education**: Educate family members about ADHD, its symptoms, and its impact. Understanding the condition helps in providing empathetic and effective support.
   - **Resources**: Utilize books, articles, and online resources to learn about ADHD. Attend workshops and seminars if available.
   - **Professional Guidance**: Involve healthcare professionals to provide education and answer questions about ADHD.
3. **Shared Responsibilities**: Distribute responsibilities within the family to reduce the burden on any one person and ensure a supportive environment.
   - **Task Sharing**: Assign tasks based on individual strengths and preferences to ensure everyone contributes and feels valued.

- o **Collaborative Planning**: Involve all family members in planning routines and schedules to ensure they are realistic and achievable.

2. Educational Support

1. **Teachers and School Staff**: Build strong relationships with teachers, counselors, and school staff. Regular communication ensures that everyone is on the same page regarding the student's needs and accommodations.
   - o **Regular Updates**: Schedule regular meetings or check-ins to discuss the student's progress, challenges, and any necessary adjustments.
   - o **Collaboration**: Work collaboratively to develop and implement Individualized Education Programs (IEPs) or 504 plans that address specific needs.
2. **Special Education Services**: Utilize special education services and resources provided by the school.
   - o **Resource Rooms**: Access resource rooms or specialized programs that offer tailored instruction and support.
   - o **Tutoring**: Consider hiring tutors who specialize in ADHD to provide additional academic support.
3. **Peer Support**: Encourage participation in study groups and extracurricular activities to build peer relationships and support networks.
   - o **Buddy System**: Establish a buddy system where students can support each other academically and socially.
   - o **Clubs and Activities**: Involve the individual in clubs and activities that align with their interests and strengths.

3. Professional Support

1. **Healthcare Providers**: Establish a team of healthcare providers, including pediatricians, psychiatrists,

psychologists, and counselors, who specialize in ADHD.

- o **Regular Check-ups**: Schedule regular appointments to monitor progress and adjust treatment plans as needed.
- o **Medication Management**: Work closely with healthcare providers to manage and adjust medications, if prescribed.

2. **Therapists and Counselors**: Engage therapists and counselors who provide behavioral therapy, cognitive-behavioral therapy (CBT), and other therapeutic approaches.

- o **Therapy Sessions**: Regular therapy sessions can help address emotional and behavioral challenges associated with ADHD.
- o **Family Therapy**: Consider family therapy to improve communication and support within the family unit.

3. **Coaches**: ADHD coaches can provide personalized strategies and support for managing daily tasks, improving organizational skills, and setting goals.

- o **Skill Building**: Coaches can help develop skills in time management, planning, and prioritization.
- o **Accountability**: Coaches provide accountability and regular check-ins to ensure progress and consistency.

4. Community Support

1. **Support Groups**: Join local or online support groups for individuals with ADHD and their families. These groups provide a platform to share experiences, advice, and encouragement.

- o **Local Meetups**: Attend local meetups or support group meetings to connect with others facing similar challenges.
- o **Online Communities**: Participate in online forums, social media groups, and websites dedicated to ADHD support.

2. **Workshops and Seminars**: Attend workshops, seminars, and conferences on ADHD to gain new insights, strategies, and connect with experts and peers.
   - **Educational Events**: Look for events hosted by ADHD organizations, schools, or community centers.
3. **Advocacy Organizations**: Get involved with organizations that advocate for ADHD awareness and support.
   - **Volunteer**: Volunteer with organizations like CHADD (Children and Adults with Attention-Deficit/Hyperactivity Disorder) to help raise awareness and support others.
   - **Advocacy**: Participate in advocacy efforts to promote better understanding and support for ADHD at the community and policy levels.

5. Building Personal Support Networks

1. **Friends and Peers**: Build a network of friends and peers who understand and support the individual with ADHD.
   - **Communication**: Be open about ADHD and its impact, fostering understanding and empathy among friends.
   - **Supportive Activities**: Engage in activities that promote positive interactions and build strong relationships.
2. **Mentorship**: Seek out mentors who can provide guidance, support, and inspiration.
   - **Role Models**: Identify role models who have successfully managed ADHD and can offer advice and encouragement.
   - **Professional Mentors**: Connect with mentors in academic or professional fields of interest.

3. **Self-Care and Well-Being**: Encourage self-care practices to maintain physical and mental well-being.
   - ○ **Healthy Habits**: Promote healthy eating, regular exercise, and adequate sleep.
   - ○ **Mindfulness and Relaxation**: Practice mindfulness, meditation, and relaxation techniques to manage stress and improve focus.

Navigating Life Stages

ADHD presents unique challenges at different life stages, from childhood through adulthood. Early identification and intervention are crucial for young children, as ADHD can significantly impact learning and development. In adolescence, the focus shifts to managing academic and social implications, as well as preparing for the transition to adulthood.

For adults with ADHD, managing workplace challenges and relationships becomes a priority. Accommodations in the workplace, such as flexible schedules and assistive technology, can enhance productivity and job satisfaction. Building strong, supportive relationships requires effective communication and conflict resolution skills.

Long-term strategies for a fulfilling life

1. Self-Awareness and Acceptance

1. **Understanding ADHD**: Continually educate yourself about ADHD, including its symptoms, effects, and how it manifests uniquely in you.
   - **Ongoing Learning**: Stay updated with the latest research, attend workshops, and read books or articles on ADHD.
   - **Personal Reflection**: Regularly reflect on how ADHD affects different aspects of your life to identify patterns and triggers.
2. **Acceptance**: Embrace ADHD as part of who you are. Acceptance is crucial for self-esteem and mental health.
   - **Positive Mindset**: Focus on the strengths and unique qualities ADHD brings, such as creativity and energy.
   - **Self-Compassion**: Practice self-compassion and avoid self-criticism. Understand that challenges are part of the ADHD experience.

2. Effective Time Management and Organization

1. **Structured Routines**: Develop and maintain structured daily routines to provide stability and predictability.
   - **Consistent Schedules**: Stick to regular sleep, work, and meal times.
   - **Morning and Evening Routines**: Establish routines that help start and end the day smoothly.
2. **Time Management Tools**: Use tools and techniques to manage time effectively.
   - **Calendars and Planners**: Utilize digital or paper planners to schedule tasks and appointments.
   - **Timers and Alarms**: Set timers for tasks to create a sense of urgency and stay focused.
3. **Prioritization**: Learn to prioritize tasks and focus on what's most important.

- **To-Do Lists**: Create daily to-do lists and prioritize tasks based on importance and deadlines.
- **Breaking Tasks Down**: Break larger tasks into smaller, manageable steps to prevent overwhelm.

3. Career and Professional Development

1. **Strength-Based Careers**: Choose a career path that aligns with your strengths and interests.
   - **Career Assessment**: Take career assessments to identify suitable fields and roles.
   - **Professional Guidance**: Seek guidance from career counselors or ADHD coaches.
2. **Workplace Accommodations**: Advocate for necessary accommodations at work to enhance productivity and job satisfaction.
   - **Flexible Work Arrangements**: Explore options like flexible hours or remote work if they improve your work performance.
   - **Assistive Technology**: Utilize tools and software designed to help with organization, time management, and focus.
3. **Continuous Learning**: Engage in continuous learning and skill development.
   - **Professional Development**: Attend workshops, take courses, and pursue certifications relevant to your career.
   - **Mentorship**: Seek mentors who can provide guidance, support, and insights into career advancement.

4. Healthy Relationships

1. **Communication Skills**: Develop effective communication skills to enhance relationships with family, friends, and colleagues.

- o **Active Listening**: Practice active listening and empathetic communication.
- o **Assertiveness**: Learn to express your needs and boundaries assertively.
2. **Building Supportive Networks**: Surround yourself with supportive and understanding people.
- o **Friendship Circles**: Nurture relationships with friends who offer positive support and understanding.
- o **Support Groups**: Join ADHD support groups to connect with others who share similar experiences.
3. **Conflict Resolution**: Develop strategies for resolving conflicts constructively.
- o **Problem-Solving Skills**: Enhance your problem-solving skills to address and resolve conflicts.
- o **Compromise and Negotiation**: Practice compromise and negotiation to find mutually beneficial solutions.

5. Physical and Mental Health

1. **Regular Exercise**: Incorporate regular physical activity into your routine to manage ADHD symptoms and boost overall health.
- o **Exercise Routine**: Find activities you enjoy, such as running, swimming, or yoga, and make them part of your routine.
- o **Active Lifestyle**: Integrate movement into your daily life, such as walking or cycling instead of driving.
2. **Healthy Diet**: Maintain a balanced diet to support brain health and manage ADHD symptoms.

- o **Nutrient-Rich Foods**: Focus on a diet rich in fruits, vegetables, lean proteins, and whole grains.
   - o **Avoiding Triggers**: Identify and avoid foods that may exacerbate ADHD symptoms, such as those high in sugar and artificial additives.
3. **Mental Health Support**: Prioritize mental health and seek support when needed.
   - o **Therapy and Counseling**: Engage in regular therapy or counseling to address emotional and behavioral challenges.
   - o **Mindfulness and Relaxation**: Practice mindfulness, meditation, and relaxation techniques to manage stress and improve focus.

6. Personal Development and Hobbies

1. **Pursue Passions**: Engage in hobbies and activities that you are passionate about.
- o **Creative Outlets**: Explore creative outlets such as painting, writing, music, or crafts.
- o **Skill Development**: Take classes or workshops to develop new skills or deepen existing ones.
2. **Goal Setting**: Set and pursue personal goals to foster a sense of accomplishment and purpose.
- o **SMART Goals**: Set SMART (Specific, Measurable, Achievable, Relevant, Time-bound) goals.
- o **Regular Review**: Regularly review and adjust your goals based on progress and changing interests.
3. **Volunteering**: Engage in volunteer work to contribute to the community and gain a sense of fulfillment.
- o **Community Involvement**: Find volunteer opportunities that align with your interests and strengths.
- o **Social Connections**: Volunteering can also help build social connections and networks.

7. Financial Management

1. **Budgeting**: Develop and adhere to a budget to manage finances effectively.
   - **Expense Tracking**: Track your expenses to identify spending patterns and areas for adjustment.
   - **Savings Plans**: Establish savings goals and plans to build financial security.
2. **Financial Planning**: Engage in long-term financial planning to ensure stability.
   - **Professional Advice**: Seek advice from financial planners or advisors to create a comprehensive financial plan.
   - **Debt Management**: Develop strategies to manage and reduce debt.
3. **Mindful Spending**: Practice mindful spending to avoid impulsive purchases.
   - **Needs vs. Wants**: Differentiate between needs and wants to make informed spending decisions.
   - **Delayed Gratification**: Practice delayed gratification by waiting before making significant purchases.

Conclusion

ADHD is a lifelong condition that requires continuous adaptation and management. By embracing strengths, implementing effective strategies, and building supportive networks, individuals with ADHD can lead fulfilling and successful lives. The journey involves ongoing learning, self-reflection, and resilience, but with the right tools and support, individuals with ADHD can achieve their full potential and enjoy a rich, rewarding life. Understanding ADHD as a dynamic and multifaceted condition is key to unlocking the possibilities it holds for personal growth and fulfillment. WE ONLY HAVE ON LIFE, LIVE IT TO THE FULLEST.

www.ingramcontent.com/pod-product-compliance
Lightning Source LLC
Chambersburg PA
CBHW061640250726

48659CB00004B/1317